The
Spirituality
of
Paul

Partnering with the Spirit in Everyday Life

LESLIE T. HARDIN

Kregel
Publications

ISBN 978-0-8254-4402-9

Printed in the United States of America

16 17 18 19 20 / 5 4 3 2 1

For my parents

Tom and Judy Hardin

who have believed in me

from the beginning

Contents

■

Acknowledgments

■

■ BOOKS, LIKE CHILDREN, ARE BEST RAISED in community. Raise children with no social interactions among others their age and they're bound to exhibit personalities that are withdrawn, self-consumed, and out of touch with reality. The same would be true of this book were it written with no communal context, no interaction from others. "Two heads are better than one, even if one is a goat's," my grandmother used to say. She was right, and I want to acknowledge the other "heads" that have kept this project from being so "gruff."

My thanks go out to Dennis Hillman and the good folks at Kregel for allowing me to work on a follow-up project to *The Spirituality of Jesus*. They have challenged me in a gracious and loving manner at every step along the way.

Several of my colleagues, students, and friends deserve mention for helping me with the manuscript at several points: Chris Arnold, Roland Howard, Rebecca Owens, Anthony Smith, and Garret Thompson. In their various ways, each of them provided research assistance and a critical eye to help me articulate my thoughts without being divisive in my language. Linda Stark and Marla Black, our librarians here at Johnson University Florida, have helped tirelessly in acquiring the necessary resources to complete this project. My wife Kara read nearly every chapter of the manuscript and offered helpful suggestions. To these, my friends and colleagues, I offer my gratitude for their collaboration on this project. Any others who were involved whom I did not mention have failed to appear here only by accident. After this book is printed, I will remember them and be grateful.

Two perfunctory matters deserve attention here, both of them pragmatic issues of communication. First, the person about whom this book is written is known in the Scriptures by two names: one Hebrew (Saul), the other Greek (Paul). In order to maintain consistency, and in order to avoid confusion, I will refer to him always as "Paul," even when referring to the Acts narrative in which his Hebrew name appears.

Second, this book is about Christian spirituality and spiritual formation, and I primarily use two terms to describe it: "spirituality" and "Spirituality." I tend to use "Spirituality" when the work of the Holy Spirit is clearly in view in my mind, and "spirituality" when a more generic inner disposition (even sometimes a disposition reflective of the Spirit) is in view.

I have kept the citations from the original Greek and Hebrew to a minimum, using them only when necessary to keep the argument flowing in a credible way. My audience was never the scholarly community, so I have tried to keep technical jargon to a minimum.

This book is dedicated to my parents, Tom and Judy Hardin. For as long as I can remember they have encouraged me to pursue my dreams and ambitions, believing that nothing was out of reach. As I have pursued those goals they have been supportive, kind, and helpful in many ways. They have demonstrated through the years a kind of faithfulness to Christ and his Church that is akin to that of Paul—fleshed out in the midst of everyday life and responsibilities. They inherited this legacy from their own parents, who were themselves pillars of holiness, friendship, and responsibility.

■

CHAPTER I

"Imitate Me":
Paul and the Practice of the Spirit

■ OF ALL THE PEOPLE IN THE NEW TESTAMENT, Paul confounds my expectations and understanding more than anyone. I understand Nicodemus—religious leader, curious about Jesus, but not wanting to get too close for fear that Jesus might just be another Satan-sent devil masquerading as an angel of light. I can identify with loud-mouthed Peter, swearing up and down that he'd never deny Jesus, only to have his failure displayed in Scripture for all eternity. I can even wrap my mind around the thief on the cross, having nowhere left to turn for hope except to the obviously innocent man crucified there beside him. These guys I understand.

But Paul frustrates me. Paul was so committed to Jesus that he seemed unwilling to compromise with those who had different ideas— even different ideas *about the same gospel*. The Judaizers in Galatia were advocating a belief in Jesus, as was Paul.[1] But he had little respect for them and told the Galatians to have nothing to do with them.

He also often seems to contradict himself. At one point he counseled young women and widows not to marry and to remain single like himself (1 Cor. 7:8), but later said, "I counsel younger widows

---

1. Of course, this is a gross simplification of the facts. Their gospel was that the realities of life in the Jewish Messiah Jesus could only be experienced as a Jew. Therefore, Gentiles needed to be circumcised and obey the ceremonial elements of Sabbath-keeping, food laws, and Jewish holy days.

to marry" (1 Tim. 5:14). At one point he told the Galatians "there is neither . . . male nor female" (Gal. 3:28), but told the Corinthians (1 Cor. 14:33–35) and Timothy (1 Tim. 2:12) that women were not permitted to teach or exercise authority in the corporate gathering of the local church. Paul spoke in tongues, apparently more than the Corinthians (1 Cor. 14:18), but downplayed tongue-speaking among them to curb its use in their assembly. He taught his converts that the Law had been "nailed to the cross" with Christ (Col. 2:14), but consistently made sure that his converts knew the Old Testament. He refused to let the Galatians be circumcised to appease Jews (Gal. 5:2), but circumcised Timothy (Acts 16:3) and shaved his own head for similar reasons (Acts 21:20–26). The more I study Paul, the more he confounds my expectations and understanding.

I'm not alone either. Peter, the apostle to whom Jesus gave the "keys of the kingdom" (Mt. 16:19) and Paul's fellow apostle, admitted that he had a hard time understanding Paul: "His letters contain some things that are hard to understand" (2 Pet. 3:16).

Of course, these dichotomies are only part of the story. The discrepancies are only *apparent* discrepancies on the surface, and any good student of the New Testament understands that behind each of the aforementioned items there were contextual, historical, and theological reasons behind Paul's actions and exhortations. Scores of books have been written on Paul and his letters, each trying to make sense of them. But the multitude of books on Paul has largely been either historical or theological. They either seek to retrace Paul's steps and illustrate his ministry against the backdrop of the Roman Empire (history), or they attempt to systematize Paul's teaching into a unified body of doctrine (theology). Both approaches are necessary, for to understand Paul we must come to grips with the world he lived in and the message with which he transformed it.

But there's another side to Paul that has been neglected. Rather than thinking of Paul as a theologian and apostle, perhaps it's time to approach Paul as a disciple of Jesus, as a Spirit-filled man practicing the Spirit as Jesus did, and as someone who lived an authentic Christian life. "Paul repeatedly emphasized the concrete shape of life in the Spirit,"[2] says Meye, and described the Christian experience as a life of "practicing the Spirit."[3] "Practicing the Spirit" is the language of spiritual discipline. So this book seeks to uncover the ways that Paul imitated Jesus in every-day appropriation of the Spirit. What were the disciplines Paul was engaged in? How did they help him in his quest to become more like Jesus? In Paul we find a true brother, a sinner who received grace, and a man honestly trying to become increasingly like Jesus (Phil. 3:7–11). Here is a man we can relate to in spirituality and Christ-likeness.

What Does It Mean to Be "Spiritual"?

Before we can begin, we must lay the foundation of what we mean by the term "spiritual," for there is great disagreement regarding the use and definition of the term. Carl Henry articulates the confusion best:

> Yet if one asks what spirituality is, one is likely to be met by a sidelong stare, as if this question would be raised only by a religious nincompoop, or could be answered by an assortment of examples without any clear definition.

> To be sure, so we are told, spirituality has something to do with spirit, but just what is intended by spirit in this context is often obscure. Talk of spirituality will evoke such identifiers as the sacred, the religious, the transcendental, the charismatic, the

---

2. R. P. Meye, "Spirituality," in *Dictionary of Paul and His Letters*, eds. Gerald F. Hawthorne, Ralph P. Martin, and Daniel G. Reid (Downers Grove, IL: InterVarsity Press, 1993), 913.
3. Ibid., 909. "Practicing the Spirit," for Paul, meant "a comprehensive pattern of action governed by one's basic perspective."

saintly, the pious. Semantic multiplication does
not stop there either. Verbally, all is fuzz.[4]

If you're confused about what it means to be "spiritual," it seems
you're in good company.

Part of the problem lies in the diverse opinion about who, exactly, takes the lead in spiritual development. Does God take the
lead, beckoning our faithful response? "We love because he first
loved us" (1 Jn. 4:19). Or does spiritual growth begin with our
own initiative, with spiritual disciplines like Bible study, prayer,
and worship, which the Spirit resonates with and rewards? Does
the effort we make provide the ideal conditions for the Spirit
to work transformation in our lives? "Come near to God and
he will come near to you" (Jas. 4:8). While Paul certainly had
religious experiences (which we will explore in just a moment),
authentic spirituality in the biblical tradition involves *more* than
experience alone and includes an element of praxis. Richard
Foster's classic, *Celebration of Discipline*, first drew our modern
attention to the spiritual disciplines as those tools which lead to
transformation. Practicing spiritual disciplines puts us in a re-
ceptive position to receive fresh "grace" from the Spirit.[5] Dallas
Willard also conceived of spiritual formation as the intertwin-
ing of grace and effort.[6] Their work has tempered our desire
for religious experience, restoring a more balanced view which

---

4. Carl F. H. Henry, "Spiritual? Say It Isn't So!" in *Alive to God: Studies in Spirituality Presented to James Houston*, eds. J. I. Packer and Loren Wilkinson (Downers Grove, IL: InterVarsity Press, 1992), 8.

5. Richard J. Foster, *Celebration of Discipline: The Path to Spiritual Growth* (San Francisco: HarperCollins, 1998), 7: "Then is it not logical to conclude that we must wait for God to come and transform us? Strangely enough, the answer is no. . . . God has given us the Disciplines of the spiritual life as a means of receiving his grace. The Disciplines allow us to place ourselves before God so that he can transform us."

6. Dallas Willard, *Renovation of the Heart* (Colorado Springs: NavPress, 2002), 22–23. For Willard, Christian spiritual formation is a "Spirit-driven process," but one that is not passive. It is a "conformity to Christ that arises out of an inner transformation accomplished through purposive interaction with the grace of God in Christ" (22).

includes our own human responsibility for spiritual formation.[7] With slight nuances of difference, these authors caution us not to put all of our eggs in the experiential basket, but to swing our pendulum back in the direction of "faithful response." Some- one must take the lead, and God acts, to be sure. Our response, then, becomes the basis of an ongoing partnership, as Evan Howard has noted: God acts, we respond, then God responds to our response.[8] This is a true give-and-take relationship between the believer and the Spirit (i.e. partnership).[9]

This idea of partnership is, in fact, exactly what we find in the biblical text regarding transformation. With deference to the problem of human responsibility and divine sovereignty, Scrip- ture consistently demonstrates that God and his people must work together to bring about personal spiritual transformation.

Probably the best (and most misunderstood) place to start is Philippians 2:12–13. Paul encourages the Philippians to "continue to work out your salvation with fear and trembling" (Phil. 2:12), but not alone, "for it is God who works in you" (Phil. 2:13). Their "accomplishing" or "production"[10] of salvation is only a faithful response to God's "working in" their hearts for his

---

7. It was this overemphasis upon spiritual *experience* to authenticate both conversion and ministry that caused early Restorationists like Barton W. Stone to return to a more biblical model (faith, repentance, confession, and baptism). For a more de- tailed accounting, see James B. North, *Union in Truth: An Interpretive History of the Res- toration Movement* (Cincinnati: Standard Publishing, 1994), 33–45; James DeForest Murch, *Christians Only: A History of the Restoration Movement* (Cincinnati: Standard Publishing, 1962), 83–96. The demand among modern evangelicals for religious experience as a necessary component of salvation in Christ was one of the main foci of Scot McKnight's addresses for the Parchman Lectures at Baylor in 2011.

8. Evan Howard, *The Brazos Introduction to Christian Spirituality* (Grand Rapids: Brazos Press, 2008), 195–228, esp. 204 ff.

9. Leslie T. Hardin, "Is a Pauline Spirituality Still Viable?" *Journal of Spiritual Forma- tion and Soul Care* 8 (2015): 132–46.

10. These are the possible ranges of meaning for "work out." See W. Bauer, W. F. Arndt, and F. Wilbur Gingrich, "*katergazomai,*" *Greek-English Lexicon of the New Tes- tament and Other Early Christian Literature*, 2nd ed. (Chicago: University of Chicago Press, 1979), 421.

will and purpose. God works in, we work out. The same partnership is articulated earlier in the letter, as Paul prays for God to increase their knowledge and understanding of the faith, expressing itself in love (Phil. 1:9), but for the express purpose of believers "discern[ing] what is best" and reckoning themselves pure and blameless (Phil. 1:10). Partnership with God is in view in Paul's letter. It is no less on display in Galatians, where Paul simultaneously prays that Christ would be "formed" within them (Gal. 4:19), while encouraging them to "keep in step with the Spirit" (Gal. 5:16, 22–25), avoid carnal living (Gal. 5:17, 19–21), and continue to do good (Gal. 6:10). Again, partnership best describes Paul's view of spirituality.

Partnership is not simply Paul's new covenant way of appropriating the Spirit. His understanding of partnership with God was developed from Scripture, including the Psalms. Those who refuse to walk in the way of the wicked and delight themselves with the knowledge of God (Ps. 1:1–3) find themselves blessed by God and afforded his protection and care (Ps. 1:3, 6). Those who have "clean hands and a pure heart" and sanctify their speech and worship (Ps. 24:3–4) receive blessing and vindication from God (Ps. 24:5), and find the privilege of standing (not kneeling or groveling) in his presence (Ps. 24:3). The renewal of the covenant in Deuteronomy 29 is based on this kind of partnering with God—the extension of the grace of the covenant by God (Deut. 29:12–13) and the faithful response of his people to abide by the terms of the covenant (Deut. 29:9, 18–28).

Jesus seems to speak about his own relationship with the Spirit in terms of partnership. Acknowledging that the Spirit was upon him (Lk. 4:18), he expressed it in tangible ways, including "preach[ing] good news to the poor" (Lk. 4:18), resisting temptation (Mt. 4:1–11; Lk. 4:1–13), and casting out demons (by the Spirit of God, Mt. 12:28). Although the Spirit is yet to come in John's Gospel, Jesus's relationship with the Father in that Gospel is described as being lived in the Spirit of God.

Indeed, the relationship between Father, Son, and Spirit in the Gospel of John (and in Jesus's life) is so intimate that articulating differences between them seems trite. Jesus sees himself sent from the Father (i.e., the Father's "apostle," or "one who is sent"), carrying out his will, serving as God's extension among his people.

So it seems best for our quest to view an authentic, biblical spirituality as a *practical partnership with the Spirit* who is already at work. The Spirit of God is at work in my heart, and the disciplines I practice set the conditions for the Spirit to have free reign in my life. Yes, Jesus is the vine, and God is the gardener (Jn. 15:1). But the disciplines I engage in till the soil and fertilize it, so that the Spirit can produce fruit in my life. This is how I see Jesus practicing his own spirituality, and the same seems to be true for Paul. It's the everyday stuff of life, done in conjunction with the Spirit and in accordance with his leading, that produces wholeness and vibrant friendship with God.

Paul, Vision, and Imitation

The problem we run up against with Paul, though, is that he was a visionary who regularly had intense religious experiences. He had visions of the Lord and of heaven, was the subject of prophecy, and often spoke in tongues. No discussion of Paul's spirituality can ignore the ecstatic experiences that accompanied his life in the Spirit. Paul's Christian life began in a vision of the risen Jesus (Acts 9:3–8, 22:6–11, 26:12–18),[11] and the Spirit continued to give him specific direction about his evangelistic ministry long after this. He was once prevented by the Spirit from

---

11. F. F. Bruce, *Paul: Apostle of the Heart Set Free* (Grand Rapids: Eerdmans, 1977), 74–75, duly noted that Paul's repeated explanation for his sudden conversion from persecutor to preacher was a claim to have seen the risen Christ. The study of the experiential aspects of the early Christian church (i.e., phenomenology) have been adequately explored by Luke Timothy Johnson, *Religious Experience in Earliest Christianity* (Minneapolis: Fortress Press, 1998).

entering Bithynia, and was instead prompted by the Spirit to go
to Macedonia (Acts 16:6–10). Jesus and the Spirit appear to him
with specific instruction or encouragement in several places in
Acts (18:9–10, 20:22–23, 23:11, 27:23–24), and by his own admission
he was given visions of things in heaven that no mortal was
permitted to speak of (2 Cor. 12:4).

But Paul also counsels his readers *against* being enamored with
ecstatic experiences. Some of Paul's opponents were using "vision"
and "revelation" to manipulate his converts into obeying ceremonial Jewish traditions. If so, then Paul's citation of Isaiah 64:4–"No
eye has seen, no ear has heard, no mind has conceived what God
has prepared for those who love him" (1 Cor. 2:9)—and his occasional statements that God is unable to be seen (Col. 1:15; 1 Tim.
1:17, 6:15–16) seem directed particularly *against* those who claim to
have had legitimate visions of God.[12] Paul himself was caught up
into the third heaven, but refused to tell what he saw there or to manipulate his readers with it (2 Cor. 12:1–10). For Paul, ecstatic experiences alone did not constitute an authentic, Jesus-style spirituality.

Here with Paul we encounter the same dilemma we encounter when ascertaining the spirituality of Jesus. Miracles, healings, and exorcisms were part of Jesus's expression of life in the
Spirit of God, but they were unique to his role as Israel's Messiah. He was uniquely indwelt by the Spirit (Lk. 4:18, 21) for a
particular role and function. I realize that speaking of it that way
brings a whole host of questions, and I have tried to deal with
them in an honest way elsewhere.[13] What is important to note
in regard to Jesus (and will most certainly help us with Paul) is
that these experiences were not the basis of Jesus's spirituality.
The foundation of his spirituality was what he did *on an everyday*

---

12. Michael Goulder, "Vision and Knowledge," *Journal for the Study of the New Testament* 17, no. 56 (1995): 63.
13. See Leslie T. Hardin, *The Spirituality of Jesus: Nine Disciplines Jesus Modeled for Us*
(Grand Rapids: Kregel, 2009), 13–25; and "The Quest for the Spiritual Jesus,"
Stone-Campbell Journal 15 (2012): 217–227.

basis: common routines like prayer, corporate worship, Scripture study, casting down temptation, etc. These everyday experiences were more normative in Jesus's life than the exorcisms, healings, and miracles—which the Gospel writers record in such detail precisely because they were so extraordinary for the covenant community. His ecstatic experiences (miracles, healings, supernatural events) were done with power freely given to him by the Spirit, and they were unique to him. I haven't been able to raise the dead or walk on water (unless it's Michigan in February), and neither have you. This kind of miraculous view of spirituality as an everyday routine is out of reach for those of us who are not gifted with the apostleship of the Twelve or given the keys to the kingdom. It's those routine disciplines of Jesus's life, not the ecstatic experiences, which call for imitation.

And so it is with Paul. Ecstatic experiences were certainly a part of Paul's spirituality, and we could make a case that they were just as normative for him as they were for Jesus. But just as the Spirit's manifestation in Jesus's life was unique to his role and purpose, so also the Spirit's manifestation in the life of Paul may have been unique to his role as apostle to the Gentiles, emissary of the risen Jesus, and founder of the new covenant community. Gordon Fee helps us understand why imitating Paul in ecstatic experiences can be problematic.

> In this context we should perhaps also include one of the dimensions of Paul's Spirituality that is most difficult to evaluate, the place of visions and revelations. We know about these only because Paul is stepping over onto the Corinthians' turf momentarily in order to persuade them that it is totally inappropriate to use such experiences to authenticate his—or anyone else's—apostleship (2 Cor. 12:1–10). What we need to note is that Paul clearly affirms that he has had such experi-

ences and apparently has had them often; but
he disallows that they have any value at all in au-
thenticating ministry.[14]

It's possible that Paul saw himself as the unique counterpart
of the Suffering Servant[15] (something to which we will return
later), and if so, the uniqueness of the Spirit's expression in
his life is commensurate with Jesus's experience. As it was with
Jesus, so it is with Paul: Ecstatic experiences, though they be
tantalizing, do not constitute the warp and woof of Christian
spirituality.

So we look to Paul's routine, everyday expressions of spirituality
to answer the question, "How can I be spiritual like Paul?" Several
times Paul tells his converts, "Imitate me as I imitate Christ" (1 Cor.
11:1; cf. Phil. 3:17, 4:9; 1 Cor. 4:16; 1 Thess. 1:6; 2 Thess. 3:7). It
seems arrogant in our individualistic society to hear someone say,
"become like I am," but it would not have been deemed so in Paul's
churches. Paul's calls to imitation are neither self-serving nor power
plays intended to marginalize those who disagree with him.[16] They
are the exhortations of a man wholly committed to Christ, calling
other believers—particularly his own converts, who knew him and
trusted him—to live in the Spirit in ways that Paul is humbly willing to model for them. We also look to Paul, not because he is a
saint, but because he knew firsthand what it meant to live life in the
Spirit, to partner with the Spirit in everyday living in order to be
conformed to the image of Christ. We look to him because he knew
what it meant to be spiritual, as Jesus was, in real and honest ways.

---

14. Gordon Fee, *Paul, the Spirit, and the People of God* (Peabody, MA: Hendrickson,
    1996), 149.
15. Ben Witherington III, *The Paul Quest: The Renewed Search for the Jew of Tarsus*
    (Downers Grove, IL: InterVarsity Press, 1998), 171–172.
16. This is the position of Elizabeth Castelli, *Imitating Paul: A Discourse of Power* (Louis-
    ville: Westminster John Knox Press, 1991), 89–136, who holds that Paul's exhorta-
    tions to imitation are nothing more than power plays, intended to homogenize the
    community of faith.

Some Limitations

We've noted that Paul was a spiritual man, and that in some respects his spirituality manifested itself in visionary and ecstatic experiences of the Spirit. But those experiences were not universally normative, and the things that call for imitation were more mundane than mystical. It's almost time to consider exactly what those routine matters were. But there are still a few things that need clarification. Before we proceed with our quest we must stop and address some idiosyncrasies of a study of this kind and, in particular, this book.

What we know of Paul's spirituality must be gleaned from Paul's Epistles and the latter half of Acts. Paul's letters contain *some* biographical references, but they are scant and occasional. Paul's purpose wasn't to write an autobiography with the hope that it would correct problems in the churches. He wrote occasional letters to the churches in order to correct their problems, and sometimes autobiographical references furthered his argument along. Add to this that it was uncustomary in the ancient world to freely talk about your own innermost thoughts and feelings, to speak in such a way as to distinguish yourself from the crowd,[17] and our quest becomes even that much more difficult. So we will have to examine the things that are plainly evident in what Paul *does*, what he *says* about life in the Spirit, and the reflection of his personal devotion that shows up in his letters.

When we refer to Paul's Epistles we specifically mean those books that bear his name in the New Testament: Romans, 1–2 Corinthians, Galatians, Ephesians, Philippians, Colossians, 1–2 Thessalonians, 1–2 Timothy, Titus, and Philemon. Savvy readers will notice that Hebrews is not included here. In spite of testimony from the early church fathers that Paul *may* have been the author,[18] and even though Hebrews bears similar linguistic style

---

17. Witherington, *The Paul Quest*, 79.
18. Eusebius says, "Paul's fourteen epistles are well known and undisputed," (*The History of the Church from Christ to Constantine*, trans. G. A. Williamson (New York:

to the writings of Paul's secretary Luke,[19] most scholars (conservative and progressive) are reluctant to attribute to Paul's hand the letter to the Hebrews.

So Where to Now?

Now that we have identified the purpose of this project and set some foundational ground rules, it's time to begin. I've identified nine spiritual disciplines in Paul's life that deserve further study and consideration of Jesus-style spirituality: prayer, evangelism and proclamation, disciple-making, corporate worship, Scripture study, holiness, caring for and building up other believers, using spiritual gifts to edify the body, and perseverance under suffering. It's not an exhaustive list, and some of the things that you might expect to find here are not developed, either because they don't receive much attention by Paul (and Luke) or because I have adequately covered them elsewhere.[20] But primary for Paul were the disciplines of prayer and evangelism. Paul was above all things a pray-er and a preacher of the gospel, and those two things often worked together to allow the Spirit to direct him where to offer the gospel next. Paul spent time in corporate worship, as was customary for ancient Jews. But Paul's discussion of worship is nuanced by the various problems he was forced to deal with among his congregants who neglected the fact that Jesus was actually present with them as they gathered. As Jesus trained disciples, so did Paul. He didn't do much

---

Penguin Books, 1965), 3.3.5), which seems to include Hebrews. He notes in that passage that some have disputed the Pauline authorship of Hebrews.

19. The suggestion that Luke may have translated Hebrews for Paul goes all the way back to Eusebius (*History of the Church* 3.38.2). Luke may have transcribed 2 Timothy at the end of Paul's life ("Only Luke is with me," 2 Tim. 4:11). J. D. Quinn, "The Last Volume of Luke: The Relation of Luke–Acts to the Pastoral Epistles," in *Perspectives on Luke-Acts*, ed. Charles H. Talbert (Danville, VA: Association of Baptist Professors of Religion, 1978), 63–67, notes several characteristics shared in common between Luke–Acts and the pastoral Epistles, which suggests that Luke may have been involved in composing them for Paul.

20. I am thinking here particularly of the disciplines of simplicity, submission, and fellowship meals. See my book *The Spirituality of Jesus*.

without taking a few people along, so we will have to spend some time discussing his habit of disciple-making.

The role of Scripture deserves significant attention in any discussion of Paul's spirituality for, as Jesus did, Paul learned it from an early age and was soaked in it. He consistently appeals to Scripture, even though his letters are primarily written to Gentiles. Holiness is expected among Paul's converts, and having been trained in holiness as a Pharisee, Paul was able to appreciate Jesus-style holiness without pushing the boundaries as far as his Jewish-Christian opponents. Paul believed that every Christian was endowed by the Spirit with spiritual gifts, and he trained his converts to use them to edify the entire church. Paul was willing to suffer for his Lord, and his discipline of perseverance in the face of suffering will yield rich application for the modern church. Finally, once we've considered what there is to know about Paul's spiritual discipline, we will be in a position to put the components all together in a comprehensive Pauline spirituality—alongside some elements of spirituality that, for whatever reason, don't find a prominent place in Paul.

I've often read the portrait of Paul in Acts and thought in surly fashion, "I wish I could be like him." Perhaps you've felt that way about him at some point or another. If so, I think that what you'll find here is encouraging and revealing, and will bring you around to the conclusion that it's possible to imitate Paul, as he imitates Christ, in living an authentic, vibrant, Spirit-filled life.

■

CHAPTER 2

"It Is Written": Paul's Devotion to Scripture

■ I WAS RAISED IN A SCRIPTURAL ENVIRONMENT. My grandfather was an elder of the local church, and frequently meditated on the Scriptures at the breakfast table. My father has served as an elder and deacon of the local church, as well as a Sunday School teacher. My parents took me to church when I was two weeks old, and for all my life, I can count on one hand the number of Sundays I haven't been in worship with the people of God. A dramatic conversion experience can't be found in my life (which prompted one fellow here in Florida to suggest to me that I might not be a Christian, or at least not a mature one!). I was born and raised in the church, baptized at the age of ten, and surrounded with Scripture by my parents and grandparents.

I remember the first Bible I ever owned. It was a small, black, leather-bound King James Version, printed on fine Indian paper, with golden tabs along the edges. The paper had a certain smell, still fragrant in my memory. I learned to read from that Bible, to study from it, and I can remember the day that it began to share space with the "updated" New International Version that my parents bought me in my teen years. I had several Bibles after those, notable among them the leather-bound NIV that now sits on my desk as a study Bible. But that small, black, leather-bound KJV gave me connections with my godly parentage. My grandfather had a big, black, leather-bound KJV that he read and studied from. The secrets of the universe were written in the margins of that book, and no presents were opened in his home on Christmas Eve until we had read the Christmas story from that Bible. True to his own heritage, my father would not permit the opening of presents on the following morning until we had read the birth narratives *again* from his own black, leather-bound KJV. I was raised in the Scriptures and, like Timothy, have known them from infancy (2 Tim. 3:15).

Of course, when I went to Bible college I was dragged to the deeper end of the pool. I was exposed to translations other than the KJV and the NIV (neither of which, I was taught, were completely accurate translations). I began to learn Greek and Hebrew, and found that some of the Scriptures permanently fixed in my mind were insufficiently translated, and needed unlearning. So I translated, all the while keeping those two primary versions handy, but carefully noting where I thought corrections needed to be made, even supplementing them in my mind with my own translations. Students sometimes find it difficult to follow along while I'm teaching, for while I primarily teach and read publicly from the NIV, I often slip in phrases from the KJV and my own personal translations.

This is not unlike the education that Paul had in the Scriptures. Having learned the Scriptures in the common dialect of his day, Paul went on to study the Scriptures in their original languages, and once he began to preach, quoted from the text frequently.

And so we now turn to Paul's devotion to Scripture. Paul was immersed in Scripture from a young age and was able to recall it at will. But for Paul, the usefulness of Scripture wasn't in proof-texting or rule-mongering. Scripture had a very practical purpose, and it had nothing to do with the acquisition of holy knowledge.

The Rabbi and the Book

Paul grew up with Scripture. As the son of a Pharisee he was educated in the Scriptures from an early age. Jewish fathers, from the time of Moses, bore the responsibility of educating their children in the Scriptures. Paul learned to recite the *Shema* (Deut. 6:4–9) twice daily,[1] which instructs parents, "These commandments that I give you today are to be upon your hearts. Impress them on your children" (Deut. 6:6–7). Parents were to answer questions their children had about the Law (Deut. 4:9, 6:20–25). They retold the story of the Exodus on the night of the Passover, answering any questions that their children had about those events (Exod. 13:8). It wasn't just in the home that Paul learned Scripture. The synagogue services of first-century Judaism and the liturgies of the major feasts in the temple were characterized by the public reading of Scripture, and Paul's repeated exposure to Scripture in synagogue and temple only helped to cement the education Paul was receiving from his godly parents.

Paul grew up in Tarsus, and learning the Old Testament outside of Judea meant learning it in Greek, not its original Hebrew.[2] At some point in his life (perhaps as a teenager), Paul moved to Jerusalem and began to study under Gamaliel, grandson of the great Hillel and the first in ancient Judaism to be given the title *Rabban* (official teacher of Judaism).[3] There Paul learned to appreciate the Scriptures in their original language (Hebrew), and learned the greater precepts of Jewish *interpretation* of the Scriptures (what Paul calls "the traditions of my fathers," in Galatians 1:14) in addition to the texts themselves. He was good at it too, for by Paul's own admission, he was "advancing . . . beyond many Jews of my own age" (Gal. 1:14).

Paul's thorough upbringing in Scripture comes through on almost every page of his letters. There's hardly a chapter that doesn't contain a quote, an allusion, or a rhetorical wink in the direction

1. James D. G. Dunn, "Prayer," in *Dictionary of Jesus and the Gospels*, eds. Joel B. Green, Scot McKnight, and I. Howard Marshall (Downers Grove, IL: InterVarsity Press, 1992), 617, suggests that by the time of Jesus and Paul, the tradition may have grown to three times daily.

2. Richard B. Hays, *Echoes of Scripture in the Letters of Paul* (New Haven, CT: Yale University Press, 1989), x–xi, points out that Paul's citations from Scripture hardly ever depend upon the Hebrew language of the Old Testament, but rather almost always come from the Septuagint (Greek translation of the Old Testament).

3. W. Bacher, "Gamaliel I," in *The Jewish Encyclopedia*, eds. C. Adler and I. Singer, vol. 5 (New York: KTAV Publishing House, 1901), 559.

of something from the Old Testament. To comb through every citation and allusion found in the letters of Paul would be cumbersome indeed. (There are more than 100 citations from, and allusions to, the Old Testament in Romans 9–11 alone.[4]) Only a passing glance at any of his letters is necessary to prove how devoted he was to Scripture. Quoting it to his Jewish readers helped explain his ministry to the Gentiles, for Israel's sacred text is full of references and hints to the time when God would include the Gentiles into his plans for Israel and her redemption.

He didn't just quote it for Jewish converts, though. There is sufficient evidence in the New Testament that Paul taught his Gentile converts the precepts of Scripture. Paul quoted a fair amount of Scripture as he outlined the gospel for the Romans, and to support his arguments he appealed to the accounts of Abraham (Rom. 4:1–3; cf. Gen. 15:1–6) and Adam (Rom. 5:12–19; cf. Gen. 3) without actually retelling the stories. We can only infer that his readers in the Roman church previously knew or had access to the Jewish Scriptures for the illustrations to be effective. The same could be said for his use of the story of Hagar and Sarah (Gal. 4:21–31; cf. Gen. 16; 21:8–21) and of Moses leading the Hebrews across the Red Sea and into the desert (1 Cor. 10:1–5). Sometimes he refers to an Old Testament concept without giving a reference or explanation, which suggests that his readers were familiar with those concepts and their supporting texts. Some examples include phrases like "the two will become one flesh" (Eph. 5:31; cf. Gen. 2:24), "every matter must be established by the testimony of two or three witnesses" (2 Cor. 13:1; cf. Deut. 19:15), "honor your father and mother" (Eph. 6:2–3; cf. Exod. 20:12), and an allusion to passages in Jeremiah and Ezekiel with the phrase "peace and safety" (1 Thess. 5:3; cf. Jer. 6:14; Ezek. 13:10–16). The Scriptures weren't just for the Jews, and they weren't for the religious class. They helped everyone in the

---

4. M. Silva, "Old Testament in Paul," in Hawthorne, Gerald F., Ralph P. Martin, and Daniel G. Reid, eds., *Dictionary of Paul and His Letters*, 634.

church, Jew and Gentile, flesh out the life of faith in Messiah Jesus, to whom the Old Testament had been pointing all along.

For Paul, the Scriptures were the conduit through which the Spirit of God did the work of conviction and of building up the church. As he convinced the church in Rome that evangelism takes place when God sends evangelists to preach the gospel (Rom. 10:14–15), he prefaced (Rom. 10:13; Joel 2:32), supported (Rom. 10:15; Isa. 52:7), and concluded (Rom. 10:16; Isa. 53:1) his entire argument with citations from Scripture. He pictured the church as a temple (particularly, the Jewish temple), being indwelt by the Spirit of God through the testimony of the prophets and apostles (Eph. 2:19–22).[5]

We must also note that Paul wasn't well-versed in only a few favored texts. A review of the citations in his letters reveals that he quoted from a wide variety of texts from Genesis, Exodus, Leviticus, Numbers, Deuteronomy, 1 Kings, 2 Samuel, Job, Psalms, Proverbs, Isaiah, Jeremiah, Hosea, Joel, Habbakuk, and Malachi.[6] His two favorite books were Isaiah and the Psalms, and he seldom quotes the same text twice. His citations are mostly from the Greek translation of the Old Testament, but sometimes reflect his knowledge of the Hebrew, and sometimes he adapts both of those traditions to communicate the text's significance to his Christian community (as when Paul morphs a text clearly referring to Yahweh to help his readers understand the exaltation of Christ: cf. Phil. 2:6–11; Isa. 45:23).[7] He's comfortable with the *sense* of the text and never built a theological argument from a particular translation.

Paul knew the Old Testament, and he knew it well. He wasn't

---

5. Though K. O. Sandnes, *Paul—One of the Prophets?* Wissenschaftliche Untersuchungen zum Neuen Testament, vol. 2, 43 (Tübingen: Mohr-Siebeck, 1991), 224–239, sees the "prophets" as Christian evangelists endowed with the gift of prophecy, not Old Testament prophets.

6. I am using the helpful chart given in Silva, "Old Testament in Paul," in *Dictionary of Paul and His Letters*, eds. Hawthorne et al., 631, as a guide.

7. C. K. Barrett, *Paul: An Introduction to His Thought* (Louisville: Westminster John Knox, 1994), 75–77, elucidates the problem of the translations Paul had access to, their various nuances, and how those nuances might have affected his readers.

a man who quoted ten verses over and over again. Rather, he was intimately acquainted with the whole of Scripture as the sacred text of God's people. And it wasn't the only thing he considered the very words of God.

Paul, Scripture, and the Jesus Tradition

Paul believed that the Old Testament was authoritative for the people of God. He taught his converts the precepts of the Old Testament, even though many of them were Gentiles. But the written Old Testament was not the only thing Paul considered authoritative, for he often appealed to the words of Jesus as an equally authoritative guide for the life of the church. By this I do not mean statements and words that Jesus spoke to Paul privately. Flip through the book of Acts in any red-letter edition of the Bible and you'll find numerous places where Jesus spoke to Paul, either at his conversion (Acts 9:4–16; 22:7–10; 26:14–18), or as a guide for his missionary activity (Acts 18:9–10; 22:18, 21; 23:11). While the words Jesus spoke privately to Paul through the Spirit are authoritative for Paul, they are not the Jesus-words I want to address here. Rather, I have in mind those statements made by Jesus during his earthly ministry that Paul's readers would have known. When settling matters of dispute, Paul pointed his readers to several of Jesus's words in the same way he pointed them to the Old Testament.

For instance, when defending his right (and that of the elders) to receive compensation for preaching the gospel, he appealed not only to the Old Testament but also to the counsel and teaching of Jesus. "For the Scripture says, 'Do not muzzle the ox while it is treading out the grain,' and 'The worker deserves his wages'" (1 Tim. 5:18). Paul's counsel here invokes the authority of the Old Testament (Deut. 25:4, "do not muzzle the ox") alongside that of Jesus (Mt. 10:10; Lk. 10:7, "the worker deserves his wages"), and labels them both "Scripture." Paul once called the high priest a "whitewashed wall," an almost verbatim quote from Jesus's accusation of the Jewish leaders as "whitewashed tombs" (Mt. 23:27; Acts 23:3). When instructing the Corinthians about the respectful observance of the Lord's Supper, Paul quoted the words of Jesus in the upper room, that this be done "in remembrance" of Jesus (1 Cor. 11:24–25; Lk. 22:19-20). He twice refers to Jesus's statements about love being the fulfillment of the entire law (Rom. 13:8-10; Gal. 5:14; cf. Mt. 22:37-40). And to correct errant ideas about the second coming among the Thessalonian believers, Paul draws their attention to Jesus's words in the Olivet discourse (Mt. 24-25), where the imagery of a thief coming unannounced and without warning (Mt. 24:43-44; 1 Thess. 5:1) prompted Paul to remind them that discussion of times and dates about the second coming are irrelevant (1 Thess. 5:1; cf. Mt. 24:36, 42, 44; 25:13). They know this "very well" (1 Thess. 5:2), for it came to them "according to the Lord's own word" (1 Thess. 4:15). Jesus's words in the Olivet discourse about the second coming and the destruction of the Jerusalem temple (first the destruction of the temple [Mt. 24:4-35], *then* the second coming [Mt. 24:36-25:46]) even form the background for the elusive "man of lawlessness" passage (2 Thess. 2:1-12).[8] Regardless of the various interpretations of this difficult text, what is important for our study here is that he invokes the words of Jesus to answer their questions. He does not turn to the Old Testament to validate his ideas about the second coming, but instead turns to the One who is coming, allowing him to speak of his own return in his own way.

One statement that seems to pit Paul against Jesus appears in 1 Corinthians 7. Giving instruction on marriage and divorce, Paul prefaces a section of his comments with the phrase, "not I, but the Lord" (1 Cor. 7:10). In the very next paragraph he gives a different piece of advice and says that it comes from "I, not

---

8. Jesus explains in the Olivet discourse that the temple will be destroyed and then the second coming will take place. Many of the "sons of lawlessness" (i.e., those without the Law, Gentiles) had tried before, and Jesus looks forward to the time when it will ultimately occur. Paul, writing twenty years before the temple's destruction, can assure the Thessalonians that the second coming hasn't happened yet because the temple is still standing, and the "son of lawlessness" to destroy it has yet to do his work.

the Lord" (1 Cor. 7:12). It's easy to read this as if the words of Jesus are commanding and authoritative while Paul's counsel is merely his opinion. But closer examination shows that the section containing the Lord's advice (about divorce and remarriage, 1 Cor. 7:10-11) can be identified as a teaching which Jesus gave his disciples during his ministry (Mt. 5:31-32; Mt. 19:4-9). This is the counsel Jesus actually gave during his teaching ministry. And while Paul offers his opinion in the next paragraph, his opinion is also authoritative, given as Jesus's apostle, and reflects godly counsel that Jesus never had occasion to address (1 Cor. 7:12-16). Paul's commands are no less authoritative than Jesus's in this instance.

And oddly enough, Paul on one occasion quotes a saying of Jesus that his listeners know well, but isn't found in the Gospels. As he met with the Ephesian elders for the last time, he encouraged them to give of themselves, as he had, following the teaching of Jesus, "It is more blessed to give than to receive" (Acts 20:35). He asked them to "remember" it, which suggests that they knew it. Paul drew upon a common saying of Jesus as an authoritative guide for how the elders ought to behave, and in this way elevated the sayings of Jesus to a level of authority that is on par with the Old Testament Scriptures.

The Purpose of Scripture

Paul was immersed in Scripture, and any time he needed authoritative proof for his claims and ideas, he returned over and over again to Scripture and to the words of Jesus. He never quoted Scripture out of context, but was always faithful to the original intent of the writers. While he quoted Scripture as the authority for his ideas, he never did so to endorse his pet projects or his own personal agenda. Paul was building the church of the living God, and his scriptural citations helped his readers understand the rebellion that exists within each of us, the solution that Christ has provided for it, and the new people of God community that is united in the Spirit. These are the themes toward which the

Old Testament points and Paul continually cited its texts to prove that, in Jesus, their fulfillment has come.

There has always been a tendency among Bible-believers to treat the text either as a collection of verses that can be extracted to prove diverse and sundry personal opinions[9] or as a code that must be painfully and meticulously broken in order to be understood. Some of the theological arguments that Christians engage in are exercises in the recitation of favored verses ripped out of context to prove one particular view. Christian literature is populated with books attempting to crack some hidden code supposedly embedded within Scripture, lost for thousands of years and now available to people living in the last days. This tendency is just as prevalent (though different) among those of us who were trained in seminary, for the work of translation and exegesis tempts us to view the text as a thing to be decoded and mastered. Scot McKnight understands the tension:

> Scripture, I sometimes have to tell myself, is not designed just to be exegeted and probed and pulled apart until it yields its (gnostic-like) secrets to those who know its languages and its interpretive traditions and who can then divulge their gleanings behind pulpits on Sunday mornings or in monographs and academic journals (very few care to read).[10]

To be sure, there are difficult things to understand in the pages of Scripture (and at least one book that may contain an insider "code"—Revelation), but Paul doesn't view the Bible that way.

Instead, Paul considers the Scriptures as a teacher (Gal. 3:24) leading us toward *holiness*. He told Timothy that the Scriptures

---

9. For a fuller discussion of the pitfalls of this kind of approach, see Christian Smith, *The Bible Made Impossible: Why Biblicism Is Not a Truly Evangelical Reading of Scripture* (Grand Rapids: Brazos Press, 2011), 1–89.
10. Scot McKnight, *A Community Called Atonement*, Living Theology, ed. Tony Jones (Nashville: Abingdon, 2007), 155.

were "able to make you wise for salvation" (2 Tim. 3:15), and that
they were "useful" toward "teaching, rebuking, correcting and
training in righteousness" (2 Tim. 3:16). They teach us about sin
(Rom. 7:7), and even the stories of rebellion contained in them
were written "to keep us from setting our hearts on evil things"
(1 Cor. 10:6). The Scriptures do not exist, in Paul's mind, either
to give us something to repeatedly exegete, to make us the New
Testament rabbis, or to give godly credence to whatever plans we
make for ourselves. The Bible is not there to give us God's approval for anything and everything we want in life. It is given to
us by the breath of God (2 Tim. 3:16) to make us holy.

That doesn't mean that Paul had abandoned his theological
training. Rather, he used that training in pursuit of his kingdom
endeavors. In one instance he draws upon the original language to
prove that the word for Abraham's "seed" was singular, and therefore referred to one person—Christ (Gal. 3:16). In the same letter,
he uses the allegorizing technique of Jewish rabbis (and possibly the
technique of his Jewish opponents) to exegete the story of Sarah and
Hagar in ways that are obvious, faithful to the text, and in support
of his argument that Christ-followers are Abraham's true descendants according to God's promise (Gal. 4:21–31). Just because the
Scriptures are given to lead us to holiness and to Christ, it doesn't
mean that we are to set aside our intellect to understand them. Neither does it mean that those who are interested in learning more
about Scripture are to forsake study of the text and its original language. These things can be helpful, but they must be done while
leading us toward holiness, not toward intellectual snobbery, and
certainly not in a way that reinforces an elitist hermeneutic. David
Alan Black puts it best: "Greek, Hebrew, and Latin all have their
proper place. But it is not at the head of the cross, where Pilate put
them, but at the foot of the cross, in humble service to Christ."[11]

---

11.   David Alan Black, *Using New Testament Greek in Ministry: A Practical Guide for Stu-
      dents and Pastors* (Grand Rapids: Baker, 1993), 21.

Paul prayed that the Philippians' love would "abound more and more in knowledge and depth of insight," but toward this end: "so that you may be able to discern what is best[12] and may be pure and blameless until the day of Christ, filled with the fruit of righteousness" (Phil. 1:9-11). His words are reminiscent of Jesus's counsel in the Great Commission—that we teach our disciples not simply to understand, but rather to *obey* (Mt. 28:20).

Paul, Disrespectful of Scripture?

Paul loved Scripture, and was the embodiment of Psalm 1: "his delight is in the law of the LORD" (Ps. 1:2). And yet there are times when Paul seems disrespectful of Scripture. Paul was devoted to Scripture and saw it as a tool to make us holy (in partnership with the Spirit). But there is also a series of statements that he makes about the Law creating sin within us (Rom. 7:8-11), leading to all kinds of rule-mongering (Gal. 5:17, 19-21), and now being superseded by the Spirit (Gal. 3:22 ff.). Doesn't that suggest that Paul believes the Scriptures *aren't* useful to us?

Paul does say those things. But in order to understand what he means by them, we must first come to terms with his definition of "the Law." There are several ways to interpret the word "law" (Gk., *nomos*) as it appears in the New Testament. Sometimes it refers to the five books of Moses, and sometimes it refers to the natural order of things (Rom. 2:14-15). But the bulk of the references in Paul to "the Law" refer to something else, which Pauline scholars have been working hard for the last few decades to clarify. Perhaps a short description of the conversation will help us understand what Paul really means.

Martin Luther saw in Romans a system of salvation by grace apart from doing penance, and since his time we've interpreted

---

12. The term used here denotes specifically a discernment about morality, determining right from wrong. See W. Bauer, W. F. Arndt, and F. Wilbur Gingrich, "*aisthēsis,*" *Greek-English Lexicon of the New Testament and Other Early Christian Literature,* 2nd ed., 25.

the phrase "works of the law" (as it appears in Paul) to refer to any kind of thing we do to earn our salvation. We are saved by grace, not by doing things (Eph. 2:8-9; cf. Rom. 3:28), and especially not by acts of Catholic-style penance. That we cannot earn our salvation, I completely agree, "For it is by grace you have been saved" (Eph. 2:8). Because of Luther's legacy we've traditionally understood Paul's phrase "works of the law" to refer to the Old Testament, and because the Old Testament is full of "rules leading to salvation," we've sometimes seen Paul as preaching *against* the Old Testament, preaching that Jews were saved by works while Christians are saved by grace.

In 1977 E. P. Sanders published his monumental work, *Paul and Palestinian Judaism*, in which he systematically showed (through massive research into the Jewish documents of Paul's day) that Jews did *not* believe they were saved by works, but were included in the covenant by the grace of God.[13] The implications were that if Jews were not saved by "works" as Luther understood it, we had to go back to Paul's day and get our minds wrapped around what he meant by "works of the law."

Once we did, we began to see something very helpful. Jews believed they were saved by grace, and (as much research has borne out for us) *maintained* their status in the covenant by doing works of piety and holiness which upheld the covenant and demonstrated to the world that they were holy, set apart as the people of God. These are the "the works which derive *from* the Law" that Jews were obligated to obey to preserve their national identity. These practices that set Jews apart from every other nation were many, but boiled down to three or four major categories: circumcision,

---

13. E. P. Sanders, *Paul and Palestinian Judaism* (Philadelphia: Fortress, 1977), called this system "covenantal nomism." In his view, "election and ultimately salvation are considered to be by God's mercy rather than human achievement" (422). If so, then Jews perform "works of the law" to *maintain their status within* the covenant, rather than as a means of *entering* the covenant. Sanders saw a distinction between "getting in and staying in" (17).

food laws, Sabbath-keeping, and the observance of special holy days. These were the things that set Jews apart from the rest of the world and made them "holy" (i.e., set apart). Therefore, when Paul speaks about "works of the law" he's primarily referring to *Jewish traditions and interpretations* of the Old Testament which foster Jewish-style holiness, the kind that separated them from the rest of the world (i.e., Gentiles). Enforcing such a system only brings death and condemnation (2 Cor. 3:7–9).

Integral to Paul's gospel was an understanding that Gentiles can be included into God's hopes for the nation of Israel *by faith*, instead of external rituals of demonstrated national piety. If the gospel is for all nations, then the practices of the Jewish nation are no longer relevant. And this understanding of "works of the law" helps us come to terms with some of Paul's statements on the issue. "We maintain a man is justified by faith apart from observing [works of Jewish-style holiness]" (Rom. 3:28). The context makes more sense now in Ephesians, where his comment that "it is by grace you have been saved . . . not by [Jewish-style-holiness works]" (Eph. 2:8–10) is then followed by his assertion that Gentiles who were once excluded from Christ are now part of the people of God (Eph. 2:11–13) because Jesus has abolished by his death this holiness code "with its commandments and regulations" (Eph. 2:15). N. T. Wright concludes this discussion for us nicely:

> [Paul] is talking about *ethnic identity*, and about the practices that go with that. And he is about to show that in the gospel this ethnic identity is dismantled, so that a new identity may be constructed, in which the things that separated Jew from Gentile (as in Ephesians 2:14–16) no longer matter.[14]

---

14. N. T. Wright, *Justification: God's Plan and Paul's Vision* (Downers Grove, IL: InterVarsity Press, 2009), 115–116.

That doesn't mean that Paul is down on holiness. In fact, some of his opponents likely feared that by relaxing these Jewish holiness commands for Gentiles, immorality would run amok and God's name would be sullied among the nations. In one of his major works on the subject, Paul clearly, through recitation of Scripture, demonstrates that no one can obey the entire code, and if you can't obey *all* of it, then you're cursed (Gal. 3:10-14). The holiness that God desires cannot be mongered by rules, and so is now produced from the heart (do you hear echoes of the Sermon on the Mount?) by the Spirit of God (Gal. 5:16-25; Rom. 6:15-23, 8:9-17). And what the Spirit does can't be regulated by "law" (Gal. 5:23).

So Paul is not disrespectful of Scripture. Paul is completely devoted to Scripture, for it is the very Word of God. His derogatory comments about "works of the law," when understood this way, help us come to terms with how Paul really felt about Scripture, how he really felt about those who twist it, and the propensity within us to create rules and systems of holiness "having a form of godliness, but denying its power" (2 Tim. 3:5).

The Key to Understanding Scripture

It's easy to look at Paul's intimate knowledge of Scripture and feel inadequate. Here was a guy who was raised on Scripture in the home, heard it proclaimed and read in the synagogue and temple, and was trained in arguably the best school of his day's Judaism. It's easy to look at Paul, preacher and apostle, and exempt ourselves from aspiring to that level of knowledge. The temptation becomes easier the older we get. Opportunities for further studies give way to the responsibilities of work and home, and the aging process begins to convince us that our mind doesn't work the way it used to. So we acquaint ourselves with a verse or two, but by and large leave the knowledge of the whole of Scripture to the trained professionals.

It doesn't have to be that way. Paul was, like each of us, a regular guy. Sure, he had some training and a Scriptural upbringing which contributed to his knowledge of the text. But there's really only one thing I see that gave Paul such intimate knowledge of the Word of God: *repeated exposure*. Paul nowhere speaks of any discipline of memorizing Scripture. He never commands it, never mentions it, and never chastises anyone who can't recall the text at will. But he knew the text. He could recall it at will, just as Jesus could, and not just the favored proof-texts. Paul knew the words, the context, the meaning, the situation, the direction toward which Scripture was pointing, and its intended goal. And he knew it because he had repeated exposure to it, from his childhood to his "college" years to his preaching and teaching as an apostle to the Gentiles. Paul knew Scripture thoroughly because he was constantly around it.

You and I have more access to Scripture than Paul ever thought about. In Paul's day paper (or papyrus or parchment) was expensive, and the copying of a single text could cost as much as a year's salary. Copies of the Scriptures weren't as available as they are today. You and I live in an age where the entire Bible is available on paper, on the Internet, and on our cell phones, in any version, in any language, and where verses can easily be found on our stationery, our calendars, and our screen-savers. Scripture has never been so readily at our fingertips, and our exposure to it has never been easier. And yet in spite of this, we're often woefully ignorant of Scripture's context and direction.

There's something that happens when you begin to devote yourself to the study of Scripture. I've noticed that my students go through the process, just as I did, and I'm confident that if you devote yourself to a lifelong study of Scripture, you'll experience much the same. It happens in three phases. The first phase happens when we don't know much about the Bible: thinking *about* Scripture. We learn the basics, see things that we have never seen before, and start to acquire a basic knowledge of what the text says. When we've done that long enough, our study begins to enter phase two: thinking *with* Scripture. In this phase, we bring the Bible alongside us in everyday matters, and consciously begin asking the question,

"What does the Bible have to say about this?" The next phase—and it only happens by being soaked in the text—is thinking *from* Scripture. At this level we've moved beyond knowing the content and the stories of Scripture and their application to our daily life. At this stage, we see all of life through the lens of Scripture. I no longer ask, "What does the Bible have to say about this?" but rather say to myself, in every area of life, "Scripture has already addressed this." Scripture before us, Scripture beside us, Scripture inside us—these are the three phases of biblical learning.

As an example: When I was first learning about the Bible, I wanted to know about the temple, so I began studying it. I learned about the Court of the Gentiles, the Court of Israel and the Court of the Priests. I learned about the Holy Place and the vessels that were used inside. I came to find out that only the High Priest went into the Most Holy Place, and only on Yom Kippur ("The Day of Atonement"). This was all stage one learning—learning *about* the temple. But later I began to enter the second stage, thinking *with* Scripture. I came to see "temple" language all over Scripture, and some of it appeared *after* the Jerusalem temple had been destroyed. That led me to a deeper understanding of the temple as the place where God dwelt and met with his people, and that now I *am* that place where God dwells (cf. Jn. 2:19-22; 1 Cor. 6:19; Eph. 2:21). That's a different kind of thinking, for now I'm taking the details I've acquired in stage one and applying them to a deeper understanding, to a kind of thinking *with* the other parts of the text that reveal God's complete thought on the subject. I saw evidence of stage three, oddly enough, when I saw the movie *Avatar*. As I watched the scene where the Earth army destroyed the Hometree of the Omaticaya, their sacred place of worship, and saw the dread on the faces of the people as it fell to the ground, my first thought wasn't to feel sorry for the fictitious people in the movie. Rather, the only thought that ran through my head was, "This must have been what it was like for the Jews when the temple was destroyed." Their sacred place of worship, their great icon of life with God, had been destroyed, and there was much dread, sorrow, and fear. I began to watch this film, not from a critique of the new-age philosophy embedded within, but rather through the lens of the experiences of those who authored the Bible. This is something of what it means to think *from* Scripture—to see everything with Scriptural eyes.

When we see Paul in the pages of the New Testament, we see him squarely rooted in the third phase. He's been so immersed in Scripture his whole life that the Word of God *drips* off him in almost every paragraph of his writing and speech. He saw everything through the lens of Scripture, and faced no problem that Scripture hadn't already addressed in some way or another.

Paul's experience isn't out of reach. Don't get discouraged if you find yourself a novice at Bible reading. Keep studying, keep learning, and keep exposing yourself to its teaching. Read it. Listen to it. Say it out loud. Memorize it. Repeat it. Write it. Translate it. Even put it in your own words. Expose yourself to Scripture repeatedly, and I guarantee that you'll find it entering your memory in a way that allows you to recall it at will. It will become an effective tool for your encouragement in the Spirit as he reminds you of what you've learned. It will also (as it did for Jesus) provide you the necessary resources to cast down temptation, enabling you to be what Paul viewed the Scriptures as intending you to be: holy.

■

CHAPTER 3

"For This Reason I Kneel":
Paul at Prayer

■ ABOVE EVERYTHING ELSE, PAUL WAS A MAN of prayer and evangelism. These are the two aspects of his spirituality that stand out more than anything else. And yet, only one—Paul's empire-wide expansion of the gospel to Gentiles—has received significant attention among biblical scholars. The deep well of Paul's devotion to prayer has remained largely untapped. Several studies have been done regarding prayer-type language in Paul's Epistles,[1] but few focus on Paul's practice of prayer itself. As Fee puts it, "Indeed, most people's understanding of Paul is limited either to Paul the missionary or to Paul the theologian. But what is clear from Paul's letters is that he was a *pray-er* before he was a missioner or a thinker."[2]

We don't have any of Paul's actual prayers. The two primary sources for the life of Paul—his Epistles and Acts—frustrate us on this. Acts is concerned mostly with Paul's evangelistic activities and God's maneuvering of Paul to preach the gospel in Rome. Though Luke mentions Paul praying on several occasions (Acts 9:9-11, 13:2-3, 16:25, 20:36, 21:5, 22:17, 28:8), he never records any of Paul's prayers. The problem with Paul's Epistles

---

1. The most notable among them are Gordon P. Wiles, *Paul's Intercessory Prayers: The Significance of the Intercessory Prayer Passages in the Letters of St. Paul* (Cambridge: Cambridge University Press, 1974); and David M. Stanley, *Boasting in the Lord: The Phenomenon of Prayer in Saint Paul* (New York: Paulist Press, 1973).
2. Fee, *Paul, the Spirit, and the People of God*, 147.

is just that—they're epistles, not biographies or prayer journals. Just as most of us don't record our most intimate prayers to God in our emails (nor have I included any in this book), Paul's Epistles don't provide us with many details of his prayer life. We have plenty of prayer-type language in Paul, even reports of prayer, but no prayers themselves.[3]

But our quest is not lost, for in the Epistles of Paul the terminology and vocabulary of prayer is overwhelming, rivaling the frequency of favored Pauline concepts like "grace," "Spirit," and "in Christ." Paul has more to say about prayer than almost any other topic. He viewed it as part of the normative experience and spirituality of every believer.

We will begin by sketching what Luke tells us of Paul's habit of prayer and note how his training in the home of a Pharisee might have influenced his prayers. Once we've set the background for Paul's prayer life, we will outline (in the tradition of Origen) the "what and how" of Paul's prayers.[4] We must consider what and who he prayed for, and why. Prayer for Paul was sometimes ceremonial and theological and at other times plain and honest. His intimacy and confidence in prayer is akin to that of Jesus, and what he prayed for just may surprise you. Once we've sketched an overall portrait of prayer in Paul's life and the Epistles, a few words of application will help us in our quest to imitate Paul in prayer.

Paul's Habit of Prayer

Paul learned to pray at an early age. His father was a Pharisee

---

3. This is a frustration noted by several major scholars in this area. Krister Stendahl, "Paul at Prayer," *Interpretation* 34 (1980): 240, counsels that we do not have any formal prayers in Paul's Epistles, only prayer-type language. See Wiles, *Paul's Intercessory Prayers*, 6–24; W. B. Hunter, "Prayer," in *Dictionary of Paul and His Letters*, eds. Hawthorne et al., 726.

4. Origen, *On Prayer*, in *Origen: An Exhortation to Martyrdom, Prayer, and Selected Works*, trans. Rowan A. Greer, The Classics of Western Spirituality (Mahwah, NJ: Paulist Press, 1979), 1.1–2 (pp. 81–84).

(Acts 23:6), and as a Jew aspiring to live the priestly life[5] his father would have passed on his piety to his son. It was the responsibility of every Jewish father to train his children in godly precepts (Deut. 6:4–9), including Scripture, obedience to the Law, and prayer. He would have learned to begin and end the day praying the *Shema* (Deut. 4:4–6), followed by recitation of the Ten Commandments and the *Amidah*,[6] a common set of eighteen formulaic prayers and blessings.[7] Paul learned these things primarily in the home and in the synagogue, where the focus was on Scripture reading and prayer.

Luke presents Paul praying in a number of venues and situations. When we first meet him, he is praying during his conversion. God told Ananias to find Paul, "for he is praying" (Acts 9:11). This prayer was accompanied by fasting, and Stanley notes that prayer may have formed the most substantial link between his old life in Judaism and his new life in Christ.[8] Paul and Silas spent a night in a Philippian jail praying. Silent prayer was not common in the ancient world,[9] so their prayers were audible, and the other prisoners were listening (Acts 16:25). Paul prayed with the elders of the church in Ephesus (Acts 20:36) and the disciples in Tyre (Acts 21:4–6) prior to his last visit to Jerusalem, knowing he would not see them again. Once he got to Jerusalem he went to the temple specifically to pray (Acts 22:17). On the island of Malta he healed the father of Publius through prayer, prompting the inhabitants of the island to flock to Paul (Acts 28:8–9). And while Luke doesn't specifically mention it, there were doubtless many nights spent in

---

5. This is how Meeks describes the intention of Pharisaism. Wayne A. Meeks, *The First Urban Christians* (New Haven, CT: Yale University Press, 1983), 97.

6. McKnight, *A Community Called Atonement*, 155.

7. For a brief introduction to the *Amidah*, with the complete text of the prayer, see Brad H. Young, *Meet the Rabbis: Rabbinic Thought and the Teachings of Jesus* (Peabody, MA: Hendrickson, 2007), 147–155.

8. Stanley, *Boasting in the Lord*, 42.

9. Pieter W. van der Horst, "Silent Prayer in Antiquity," *Numen* 41 (1994): 1–25. Silent prayer in the ancient world was used primarily to keep one's enemies from hearing the petition (presumably because you were praying *against* your enemies).

prayer during Paul's difficult sea voyage to Rome—a trip that Luke indicates was fraught with danger at every change of wind direction. This is the portrait that Luke gives of Paul the pray-er, praying at nearly every turn of the page, in a wide variety of contexts.

The Freedom to Pray

The variety that Paul demonstrates in prayer isn't solely a matter of context, though. He prays in a variety of situations, but also with a depth and richness of vocabulary. As we search through the Epistles for evidence of Paul's practice of prayer, the first thing that overwhelms us is the sheer amount of evidence. Though there are no actual prayers, Paul is constantly talking about and calling for prayer. The references to prayer are overwhelming, as is the breadth of vocabulary used to describe it.

Because of his theological training, we expect to find ceremonial and liturgical prayers in theological language, and indeed we do. Paul prays sometimes in the exalted language that he learned as a Pharisee. One example of this are the doxologies ("short, spontaneous ascriptions of praise to God")[10] such as "To our God and Father be glory forever and ever. Amen." (Phil. 4:20; cf. Rom. 9:5; 2 Tim. 4:18). A great example is found in Ephesians 3:20-21: "Now to him who is able to do immeasurably more than all we ask or imagine, according to his power that is at work within us, to him be glory in the church and in Christ Jesus throughout all generations, for ever and ever! Amen." (cf. Rom. 11:33-36, 16:25-27; 1 Tim. 6:15-16). These are the kinds of prayers often uttered in the synagogue, and Paul transformed them into statements of praise and glory to God on behalf of his gift of grace in Christ Jesus.

But Paul didn't always pray in the exalted language of his training. Jesus prayed in ordinary, everyday language; Paul fol-

---

10. P. T. O'Brien, "Benediction, Blessing, Doxology, Thanksgiving," in *Dictionary of Paul and His Letters*, eds. Hawthorne et al., 69.

lowed suit, refusing to imbue prayer with only elitist vocabulary. He often called his readers simply to "prayer," a term quite generic and readily understood by both Jews and Gentiles.[11] He also prayed with "petitions" addressed to the Father (Eph. 6:18; Phil. 1:4, 4:6; 1 Thess. 3:10; 2 Tim. 1:3) and "requests" like those addressed to a king[12] (Rom. 8:27; 1 Tim. 2:1, 4:5). Paul even finds the freedom to "plead" with or even "exhort" (2 Cor. 12:8)[13] and "challenge" the Father (Phil. 4:6; Col. 1:9).[14] Scholars from all stripes have long noted that even his wishes seem like prayers,[15] so that a wish-type statement to the Corinthians that God "will keep you strong to the end" (1 Cor. 1:8) comes across as "I pray that God will keep you strong." Paul will not let prayer degenerate into simple asking, though, as if God were a spiritual vending machine. The language of "thanksgiving" is the most frequent of all the prayer vocabulary in Paul's Epistles. He thanks God often for his converts (1 Cor. 1:4; Col. 1:3; 1 Thess. 1:2–3; Eph. 1:16; Phil. 1:3; 2 Tim. 1:3) and for the grace of God in Christ (2 Cor. 9:15; cf. 1 Cor. 15:57), and challenges his readers to do the same (Eph. 5:4; Col. 1:12, 2:7, 3:15, 4:2; 1 Thess. 5:18).

---

11. Hunter, "Prayer," *Dictionary of Paul and His Letters*, eds. Hawthorne et al., 730.
12. O. Bauernfeind, "*tugchanō, ktl.*," *Theological Dictionary of the New Testament*, eds. G. Kittel and G. Friedrich, trans. G. W. Bromiley, 10 vols. (Grand Rapids: Eerdmans, 1964–1976), 8:244.
13. This is frequently the term used to denote exhortation in the New Testament (*parakaleō*).
14. G. Stählin, "*aiteō, ktl.*," *Theological Dictionary of the New Testament*, 1:191–193. Stählin notes that this term has an overarching connotation of "demanding for one's self," and that Jesus never used this in his own prayers. Though the vocabulary is different (*erōtaō*), William David Spencer and Aida Besançon Spencer, *The Prayer Life of Jesus: Shout of Agony, Revelation of Love, a Commentary* (Lanham, MD: University Press of America, 1990), 115–117, suggest that Jesus used it in the sense of "challenge."
15. These "wish-prayers" are not Paul's way of manipulating the future, but simple assertion, based on his knowledge of God and his promises, of what God already intends to do among his people. They serve both as confident reminders to his readers and prayers to God that he will indeed fulfill those promises. See also similar statements in 2 Corinthians 9:11, 13:11; Romans 16:20; and Philippians 4:19.

If Paul's example tells us anything, it's that he felt the freedom to pour out his heart before the Father. Sometimes he
prayed with the theological language he learned as a Pharisee.
At other times his prayers were expressed in everyday vocabulary. He was genuine, honest, and comfortable, even when he
prayed from his theological background and knowledge. In this
he imitated Jesus, whose address of God as "Abba" was not to be
equated with "Daddy," but still denoted more familiarity than
was customary.[16]

So the language Paul used for prayer was rich and varied, diverse and nuanced, and it revealed that Paul's relationship with
the Father was, like that of Jesus, very intimate. He could both
praise the Father in blessing and present his honest, heartfelt requests to his King as a trusted friend. I suspect that, given what
Paul teaches about prayer and his profound allegiance to the Lord
Jesus, that his prayers were intense but respectful. The "confidence" Paul found to preach Christ (*parrēsia*; sixteen times this
word is used in the NT to describe Paul's preaching) also led to a
confidence or "boldness" before the Father (Eph. 3:12), to a freedom in prayer that was honest and intimate, yet respectful.

The Content of Paul's Prayers

Now that we've examined the vocabulary that Paul used in his
daily conversations about prayer, and seen the freedom that he felt
in the presence of the Father, it's time to turn to a consideration of
the kinds of things Paul prayed for. What he prayed for—and didn't

---

16. Contrary to popular opinion, "Abba" is not the equivalent of "daddy." It is the
    respectful term Jesus used to address God (Mk. 14:36), and while it was familiar,
    it was intensely respectful. The seminal article on this is by James Barr, "Abba Isn't
    'Daddy'", in *Journal of Theological Studies* 39 (1988): 28-47. See also corroborating
    comments by James D. G. Dunn, *Jesus and the Spirit* (Philadelphia: Westminster,
    1975), 22-24. Stendahl, "Paul at Prayer," 245, n. 13 cautions that "the romantic
    interpretation of *Abba* as an endearing term for God, with the informal and familial
    connotation of 'Dad' rather than 'Father,' is presumably without firm foundation."

pray for—involved higher and more kingdom-minded things than most of us were taught.

Praying for Others

Paul prayed fervently for his converts and the congregations under his care. In several places he mentions that he and his companions prayed for them, with no specific content mentioned other than an occasional "remembering you in our prayers" (Eph. 1:16; cf. Rom. 1:9–10; Eph. 3:14; Phil. 1:4–5; Col. 1:3; 1 Thess. 1:2; 2 Thess. 1:11). In a very real way Paul felt the connection between himself and these converts through the Spirit of God, so that even when he was physically absent from them the connection was not severed (1 Cor. 5:4; Col. 2:5).

What Paul asked God for most was their continued *growth in the faith*. Having been torn from Thessalonica so quickly, Paul earnestly prayed that he, Silas, and Timothy could return there and finish the work they began (1 Thess. 3:10). He continued to pray that God would count them worthy of the calling they had received in Christ (2 Thess. 1:11; so too the Colossians, Col. 1:10). For the Ephesians, he prayed that God would strengthen them with power in the Spirit for the indwelling Christ to continue to increase their love (Eph. 3:16–17). He prayed for the Corinthians' "perfection" or "maturation"[17] (2 Cor. 13:9) in the faith. Paul prayed that Philemon would be active in sharing his faith, for only then would Philemon know the true meaning of what was his in Christ (Phm. 6).

The growth Paul hoped for in his disciples was tied to knowledge and wisdom, and particularly their insight into the vast nature of God's grace. So he continually prayed for the believers at Ephesus, that God would give them wisdom and revelation,

---

17. The word Paul uses here has more a sense of maturation than perfection. See W. Bauer, W. F. Arndt, F. Wilbur Gingrich, and F. W. Danker, "*katartisis*," *Greek-English Lexicon of the New Testament and Other Early Christian Literature*, 3rd ed. (Chicago: University of Chicago Press, 2000), 526.

that their eyes might be open to see the reality of the depth of God's love (Eph. 1:17–19), a prayer similar to what he offered on behalf of the Colossians (Col. 1:9). This "knowledge and depth of insight," however, was no esoteric head-knowledge. For Paul, it involved the ability to flesh out God's will in holy living once it was understood properly (Phil. 1:9).

In return, Paul expected his disciples to devote themselves to praying for one another. They were to "keep on praying for all the saints" (Eph. 6:18), knowing that others were praying for them (2 Cor. 9:14). Whether it was for knowledge, insight, or intercession for Paul or one another, he expected them to "pray continually" (1 Thess. 5:17) and to "devote yourselves to prayer" (Col. 4:2; cf. Rom. 12:12).

Praying for Himself

Paul also felt the freedom to pour out his own wants and desires before the Father. His practice reminds us that prayer is not about juggling the right theological vocabulary, nor is it about saying the right "magical" words to get the Father's attention. It was Paul's relationship with the Father, through the Spirit, that gave Paul the freedom to approach the throne of God in confidence, as a trusted friend. In this he imitated Jesus, whose most heartfelt desires were free to be expressed in the Garden of Gethsemane.

Most of Paul's personal desires in prayer were related to his travel itinerary. Paul's most fervent petition in prayer was bound up with the next steps for his evangelistic ministry.[18] The Spirit was orchestrating Paul's travels, sometimes allowing him to stay where he was (Acts 18:9–10), and at other times preparing open doors into untapped locations (1 Cor. 16:9; 2 Cor. 2:12). After Paul articulated his desire to preach the gospel in Rome (in-

---

18. Stendahl's discussion of this aspect of Paul's prayer life is most fascinating. See his "Paul at Prayer," 242–244.

deed, he prayed for it: see Rom. 1:10–13, 15:23–32), the Spirit of God made it possible, though not in ways that Paul had envisioned (i.e., as a prisoner). While Paul was afraid for his life in Jerusalem, the Spirit reassured him that he *would* preach in Rome (Acts 23:11), and appeared to him during a fierce storm on the way to reassure him of his safety (Acts 27:23–24). These intense experiences, sometimes visionary, seem always to have been bathed in prayer for the appropriate direction for his travels. Prayer (with fasting) was the occasion for the Spirit to set aside Paul and Barnabas for evangelistic mission in the first place (Acts 13:2–3), and it seems that Paul leaned on the Spirit in prayer to direct him in his journeys.

Paul didn't always get his way, though. Sometimes the Spirit *prevented* Paul from doing ministry in particular locations. At one point Paul wanted to do mission work in Bithynia, but was prevented by the Spirit from doing so, and was instead directed toward Macedonia (Acts 16:6–10). Twice he told the Romans that he had been prevented from coming to them (Rom. 1:13, 15:22). In neither of these contexts are his enemies in view, but only Christ Jesus, suggesting that it was the Spirit of Christ who was directing his travels.

So what is it that Paul prayed for? Most of the requests he makes on his own behalf come round to *categories framed and shaped by the gospel.* Even when he prays for deliverance and safety, the ultimate goal is "that the message of the Lord may spread rapidly and be honored" (2 Thess. 3:1), that God would open up new doors of opportunity for evangelism (Col. 4:3), and that when these become available, that he would declare the mystery of the gospel fearlessly (Col. 4:4; Eph. 6:19–20). He fully expected to find the strength to do so (Phil. 1:20). Here his two overarching passions—prayer and evangelism—converge for a common purpose.

Wrestling with the Spirit: Paul Struggling at Prayer

Paul was completely respectful in prayer, ascribing glory and majesty to the God he'd known since birth, laying his requests before the Father as before a king. But prayer for Paul wasn't all pomp and circumstance, ceremony and liturgy. Paul often struggled in prayer. In this he was no different than his Lord Jesus, who genuinely struggled to do the will of God on the night of his arrest (Mt. 26:39, 42, 44). We have already noted Paul's wrestling with the Spirit over his evangelistic ministry above. But there is more to Paul's struggle than simply discerning the next preaching event. He struggled with some serious personal issues and was not afraid to hash them out with the Father.

The clearest example of Paul's struggle in prayer is bound up with his thorn in the flesh. Paul only mentions it in 2 Corinthians 12:7-10, is quite vague about it, and scholars are no closer to a consensus.[19] Paul didn't feel it was necessary to tell. The exact identification of this malady is not as important for our purposes as is Paul's "pleading" with the Lord to have it removed. He pleaded or "exhorted" the Lord to take it away from him three times, but was summarily denied (2 Cor. 12:8). That Paul felt he could approach the Father in this manner twice more after being denied the first time suggests a freedom and confidence in prayer akin to the kind that Jesus demonstrated in the Garden of Gethsemane.[20]

Paul expected that this kind of struggling in prayer would be common for believers. He mentions Epaphras, who was always "wrestling in prayer" for the Colossians (Col. 4:12). The

---

19. Eyesight, illness, defective speech, or even epilepsy are the front-runners. Bonnie Bowman Thurston, "Paul and the Mystery of Prayer," *Stone-Campbell Journal* 11 (Fall, 2008): 227, suggests that Paul's "thorn" may have been an enemy, a person, as in Numbers 33:55 (LXX) and Ezekiel 28:24. Paul Barnett, *The Second Epistle to the Corinthians*, New International Commentary on the New Testament (Grand Rapids: Eerdmans, 1997), 568-570, also hints in this direction, pointing toward the Judaizers who caused Paul so much trouble.

20. J. W. McCant, "Paul's Thorn of Rejected Apostleship," *New Testament Studies* 34 (1988): 571, notes several similarities between Paul's three-fold request to have his "thorn" removed and Jesus's three-fold request to have his "cup of suffering" removed.

term "wrestling" comes from the Greek stadium and has in the background connotations of conflict—or in a speech-act, debate.[21] Paul uses the same term as he calls for the Romans to join him in his "struggle" of prayer (Rom. 15:30). And in the struggle that continually takes place between believers and the dark forces of the unseen realm, prayer is what we do to take our stand (Eph. 6:10–18).

Prayer is not always easy. It wasn't for Paul, and it isn't for us. Paul knew this personally, and assured his readers that though we groan inwardly (2 Cor. 5:2–3), and struggle to articulate the right words in prayer (Rom. 8:26), God has not left us to fend for ourselves. The Spirit of God helps us (Rom. 8:26–27), and so does Christ Jesus (Rom. 8:34). Our frail humanity sometimes inhibits clear articulation, and we struggle for the right words. But the indwelling Spirit of God provides us with an intimate connection with the Father, so that a veil shielding us from God's glory is no longer necessary (2 Cor. 3:12–18). We can see him not as the great and powerful Oz, hiding in smoke and fire, but can approach him as his children, crying out, "Abba, Father" (Rom. 8:15–16).

Praying Like Paul

Prayer inundated Paul's letters and his life. Reports of prayer and "prayer-type language" may be the only signs that appear in Acts and Paul's Epistles, but they are the low-lying, abundant fruit of a very extensive root system in Paul's spirituality. There is much evidence for prayer in Paul's life and letters, and there are still issues that we have left untouched. If anything, I hope that what shows through in this brief discussion is that, as much as anything else, Paul was a man of prayer. Not only did he pray for his converts, but in turn taught them to pray for him and for one another. And while he was not afraid of ecstatic experiences like

---

21. E. Stauffer, "*agōn, ktl.*," *Theological Dictionary of the New Testament*, ed., Kittel 1:134–140.

speaking in tongues (1 Cor. 14:18), his prayers were dominated not by the ecstatic, but by simple thanksgiving and requests for the advancement of the gospel. After considering Paul's practice of prayer, two conclusions stand out and may help us in our quest to pray like Paul.

First, Paul helps us answer the practical yet theological question, "To whom do I pray?" For Old Testament Jews, the answer was simple: Yahweh, the one true God. But with the advent of Jesus Christ, God's son, whom the Scriptures tell us is himself God and the very nature of God (Jn. 1:1, 18; Col. 1:15; Phil. 2:6), we sometimes wonder exactly to which personage in the Trinity we should address our prayers. Paul addressed prayers to the Father, as Jesus did, but also taught that both the Son and the Spirit intercede on our behalf (Rom. 8:26, 34). In the book of Acts both the Father (Acts 4:24, 8:24, 10:2, 16:25) and Jesus (Acts 7:59) are addressed in prayer. One thing that stands out: The Spirit is never addressed in prayer. While I agree with Felicity Houghton that the lines of distinction often bleed over in prayer,[22] I am still more comfortable, because of the biblical evidence, in imitating both Jesus and Paul by directing my prayers toward the Father. It provides continuity with the Scriptures (both Old and New Testaments), the example set for us by Jesus, and the experience of the apostles.

Second, Paul's prayers are characterized by a *focus upon the kingdom of God* rather than his own wants and needs. If we're honest with ourselves, too many of our prayers are about selfish wants and needs, and often "whatever we need and want and feel forms the divine control center of our lives."[23] There is not

---

22. Felicity B. Houghton, "Personal Experience of Prayer I" in *Teach Us to Pray: Prayer in the Bible and the World*, ed. D. A. Carson (Grand Rapids: Baker, 1990): 300–301: "But who does the talking? Paradoxically, I have learnt from the Word and in my own experience that it is I who do it, and yet it is not I. It is Another. We pray, and yet when we do so truly, it is 'in the Holy Spirit' (Jude 20). . . . Prayer is therefore a mysterious co-operation between us and the Holy Spirit."

23. Eugene H. Peterson, *Eat This Book: A Conversation in the Art of Spiritual Reading*

a shred of evidence in Paul's practice or teaching of prayer for temporal, daily comforts such as improved health or economic prosperity. In fact, Paul's attitude to such things was "if we have food and clothing, we will be content with that" (1 Tim. 6:8). Paul's prayers seem primarily concerned with the gospel—where he will preach it next, how his converts can grow in it, and that he will be bold and fearless to preach it—and not with his own comfort. It's possible that he prayed for daily things like his own wants and needs, for Jesus taught his disciples to do so (Mt. 6:9-13; Lk. 11:2-4). But these kinds of requests do not find a prominent place in Paul's prayer language.

Paul's selfless discipline in prayer seriously challenges me. The first year I ever kept a prayer journal I got to the end of it and decided to leaf back through it, noting where God had answered my prayers. The exercise was helpful but not pleasant, for instead of discovering where God had met my requests, I was confronted with how frequently the pronouns "I" and "me" appeared in my prayers that year. It was eye-opening, and it changed the way I prayed. It's human nature to spend a lot of time on ourselves, asking for our own wants and needs. Part of Paul's teaching, however, is that the Spirit helps us overcome our human nature (Rom. 8:5-17; Gal. 5:13-25) so that we can focus on becoming who God intends us to become. Perhaps it's time to imitate Paul, who "urges believers to live (and pray) in ways which give first priority to the values of the present and coming kingdom."[24]

(Grand Rapids: Eerdmans, 2006), 32. Though note that Peterson was contrasting those things with the way we view and use Scripture, not prayer.

24. Hunter, "Prayer," eds. Hawthorne et al., 734.

■

CHAPTER 4

"Entrust These Things to Reliable Men": Disciple-Making

■ ONE OF MY GREAT JOYS IN MINISTRY has been to mentor disciples and co-workers for the kingdom. Genuine ministry, the kind in which the minister is involved in the lives of the people, fosters a kind of partnership that leads to long-lasting friendships and sometimes student-teacher training for future endeavors. I've served churches in Ohio, West Virginia, Michigan, and Florida, and in each of those ministries I encountered men and women whom I consider disciples and co-workers.

They appear in a variety of contexts. Some I selected to train for specific tasks in kingdom ministry, like the men I mentored in basic teaching techniques for Bible study, and the young people I trained as a worship leaders. Others were disciples in the truer sense— those who learned from me how to grow in Christ, both doctrinally and spiritually, and whom I spent considerable time shepherding and training for ministry. These are the ones Paul would have addressed with affectionate terms like "fellow soldier" and "co-worker." One of those men still signs his e-mails to me "your fellow worker."

There were still others, to me a very special class of people (both men and women), who *partnered* with me in kingdom ministry. They are the ones who would have gotten along fine without me and would have done significant kingdom things in my absence. I was the one privileged to serve beside them as partners. This last group (and I would love to name them, were I confident

I would leave none out) included those who served me as much as I served them, and the motivation to overcome the pressures and temptations of ministry came largely from folks like them. I still count them among my own fellow workers and am honored to have had the privilege of serving beside them.

There were also a few who abandoned me, or the faith (or both), and not always for reasons that were clear to me at the time, if ever.

This was not unlike Paul's experience, for Paul too had his converts, disciples, and fellow workers. Part of Paul's everyday business was to train, disciple, and mentor others to carry on his work. Paul instructed Timothy to "entrust to reliable men" that which Paul had passed on to him, with the hopes that they, in turn, would pass it on to their disciples (2 Tim. 2:2). The Pauline literature is filled with references not just to converts that Paul made and people he wanted to greet at the end of his letters,[1] but to many whom Paul trained to be his partners in preaching the gospel. And yet, not even Paul was successful in every case, for several people who were his allies deserted either him or the gospel (or both). As Paul was not shy about mentioning those who deserved honor, neither was he reticent to mention those who had abandoned, mistreated, or misrepresented him.

In the pages that follow we pause to consider Paul's routine practice of training others to carry on his work. Paul took his cues from Jesus, who trained the Twelve to carry on his work. Like his Lord, Paul was regularly engaged in training others to stand in his place and speak for him. A brief review of discipleship in Paul's world is in order before we proceed, and that must be set against the clues in Paul's letters about his methods for discipling others. We will then pause to reflect upon those whom Paul mentions as his apprentices and co-workers in the gospel. Considering Paul's

---

1. E. E. Ellis, "Coworkers, Paul and His," in *Dictionary of Paul and His Letters*, eds. Hawthorne et al., 183, mentions that there are more than 100 names associated with Paul in Acts and the Epistles. The number is significantly less once we begin to restrict the pool to those who served and traveled with Paul.

discipling activities and methods will then give us an opportunity to reflect upon the modern practice of discipleship and make points of comparison.

Ancient Discipleship and Paul's Methods

. The term "disciple" is absent from the Pauline literature. Paul did not prefer the term "disciple" for those training with him. He refers to them as "co-workers," "fellow soldiers," even "loyal son(s)," but does not call them disciples. In fact, the only "disciples" mentioned in connection with Paul are those who lowered him over the wall in Damascus (Acts 9:25)—but this is Luke's designation, not Paul's. There is some evidence that the term "disciple" in the Greco-Roman world denoted those who paid for learning, such as the students of Protagoras who were charged stiff fees for sitting at his feet.[2] Whether Paul wanted to avoid connotations of paid service in the gospel (he is vitally concerned about this elsewhere in his ministry[3]) or simply preferred to be more endearing, he found other terms more helpful to describe those closely associated with him, such as "apprentices" and "partners."

Paul's *modus operandi* for training was *time on task*. Discipleship in the ancient world was a daily affair. There was no systematic program for making disciples—no series of classes to take, no certifications, no small-group programs growing and multiplying. In the ancient world, disciples were made by *spending time with the teacher*. The great rabbis of Judaism often trained their disciples or students in the context of daily life: the master taught while the disciples did chores.[4] They served their teachers in menial tasks, for by doing so they learned how to flesh

---

2. See W. Bauer, W. F. Arndt, and F. Wilbur Gingrich, "*mathētēs*," *Greek-English Lexicon of the New Testament and Other Early Christian Literature*, 2nd ed., 419–421.
3. Paul notes carefully in several places that he worked hard so as not to entwine the gospel with the appearance of financial gain: Acts 18:3, 20:33–35; 1 Cor. 4:12, 9:6–14; 2 Cor. 6:5; 1 Thess. 2:9; 2 Thess. 3:7–8.
4. Young, *Meet the Rabbis*, 30.

out their studies. This too was the pattern for Jesus and the Twelve. They abandoned their livelihood to spend their time with him, and in doing so received intensive training to lead the early church. Paul and his disciples also followed this pattern, for several of his apprentices gave up their daily existence to travel with him, to preach the gospel, and to assist him in doing the work of the kingdom. We know that Paul was an artisan, for Luke describes him as a "tentmaker," a term that probably signifies someone who was skilled at leather-working.[5] In several passages he boasts of his hard work and labor during his preaching campaigns, suggesting that he was active in working to support himself.[6] It would have been natural for Paul to use the artisan shop as a place of discipleship, training co-workers and doing the work of evangelism as opportunities arose, even if it meant delaying his own work into the evening.[7]

This method of disciple-making was incredibly successful, for there are more than 100 individuals connected to Paul's ministry in the New Testament, and while not all of them are immediate disciples or apprentices, the number of those that are is enough to make a solid case. Paul trained apprentices as part of his routine partnership with the Spirit, and in doing so ensured that the orthodox faith would be passed to generations beyond his own.

Paul's Disciples

What strikes me more than anything as I peruse the list of Paul's disciples is that they come from all walks of life, from all

---

5. P. W. Barnett, "Tentmaking," in *Dictionary of Paul and His Letters*, eds. Hawthorne et al., 925–927; R. F. Hock, *The Social Context of Paul's Ministry* (Philadelphia: Fortress, 1980), 20–25.

6. See the references in footnote 3 above.

7. R. F. Hock, "Paul's Tentmaking and the Problem of His Social Class," *Journal of Biblical Literature* 97 (1978): 560, n. 31, lists several citations from the Greek and Roman philosophers that demonstrate the intellectual discourse plied in the first-century artisan shop. It was not simply a place for working, but a place for learning, discussion, and debate. See also Hock, *The Social Context of Paul's Ministry*, 31–33, 37–42.

backgrounds, and with a variety of gifts at their disposal to be used in service of the kingdom. Jesus chose men from a variety of contexts, having in his company of close apprentices common fishermen (Peter, Andrew, James, and John), a wealthy tax collector (Matthew), and a Zealot (Simon).

Paul followed suit, and welcomed anyone as a disciple who showed a willingness to forsake all for the work of the kingdom. Many of these apprentices were Jews, with whom Paul found a common faith in Jesus as Israel's promised Messiah. Among the Jews was Barnabas, a Levite from Cyprus (Acts 4:36) who was well-respected among the church leaders in Jerusalem (Acts 9:26–27). Silas was a Jew who may have enjoyed Roman citizenship (Acts 16:20, 37) and was respected enough by the Jerusalem Council to carry its decree to Antioch and explain it (Acts 15:23). Apollos was a Jew from Alexandria, is designated a "learned man" (Acts 18:24), and may have been formally trained in rhetoric.[8] So far it looks like a *Who's Who in Judaism*. But Paul wasn't an elitist, for he also took on disciples of the lower classes. Notable among them are Priscilla and Aquila, leatherworkers from the artisan class like Paul. They were displaced from Italy when Claudius ordered the expulsion of all Jews from Rome (even Jewish-Christians; c. 49–50 AD), and fled to Corinth where they met Paul, probably in his shop (Acts 18:1–4). Paul's influence flows through them to Apollos (Acts 18:24–26). Timothy had both Jewish and Greek ancestry (Acts 16:1; 2 Tim. 1:5, 3:14–15), and was the living embodiment of Paul's message that salvation in Christ Jesus transcends Jewish-Gentile divisions (Gal. 3:28; Col. 3:11).

True to his own message, Paul refused to train only fellow Jews, so Gentiles are also counted among his fellow workers in the king-

---

8. Apollos is described as an *anēr logios* ("learned man"). Meeks, *The First Urban Christians*, 61, suggests that this phrase indicates that Apollos had formal training in rhetoric, adding to his prowess as a preacher of the gospel. He is described as a "powerful" (*dynatos*) expositor of the Old Testament (Acts 18:24), and "one who shows" or "demonstrates" (*epideiknys*) the Scriptural proof of his arguments (Acts 18:28). For more on the terms and their meanings, see B. B. Blue, "Apollos," in *Dictionary of Paul and His Letters*, 37–39.

dom. Most notable among them was Titus, a Greek (Gal. 2:3) whom
Paul frequently sent out in his stead to places like Corinth (2 Cor.
7:13-16, 8:6, 16-21), Crete (Titus 1:5), and Dalmatia (2 Tim. 4:10).
Luke was a "doctor" and "dear friend" to Paul (Col. 4:14), and once
he began to accompany Paul, stayed with him through the rest of
Paul's life.[9] Epaphras was a Gentile, and one of Paul's "fellow work-
ers" (Col. 4:10-12). He was instrumental in preaching the gospel to
the Colossians (Col. 1:7-8) and wrestled in prayer for believers in
Asia Minor—specifically those in Colossae, Laodicea, and Hierapolis
(Col. 4:12-13). There were Aristarchus and Gaius, along with Sopa-
ter and Secundus of Thessalonica (Acts 20:4), and Trophimus the
Ephesian (Acts 20:4, 21:28-29), all of whom took up traveling with
Paul, learning the art and joy of kingdom proclamation.

These are just a few. Space does not permit me to fully describe
the backgrounds of every single person connected to Paul. And
there are likely more than those named in the New Testament.
What is evident from this short list, however, is that Paul made
disciples. He intentionally identified willing participants in kingdom ministry, brought them along, spent time with them, trained
them, and when they were ready, sent them out to do the work that
he had been doing. All of this is very much in line with the way
Jesus gathered disciples around him, spent time with them, trained
them, and sent them out to preach (Mt. 10:1-42; Lk. 10:1-24).

The Work of Paul's Disciples

Not only do they come from all walks of life, with various
backgrounds, but also with various gifts utilized for a variety of
different ministry tasks and functions. As Jesus took those in his

---

9. Luke begins to follow Paul in Acts 16:10, where the author (traditionally Luke) begins
speaking in the personal pronoun "we." Luke accompanied Paul through the second
missionary journey, all of the third, the journey to Rome, and the duration of his first
imprisonment. He seems to have accompanied Paul on segments of the journey that
others were not permitted to join (cf. Acts 20:4-6). He stayed with Paul during both
his first (cf. Col. 4:14; Phm. 24) and second (2 Tim. 4:11) imprisonments.

company and melded their background with their gifts and training, so Paul trained those in his company for a variety of tasks that were beneficial to his program of introducing men and women to Christ Jesus and helping them to mature in the Spirit.

He trained some of them to *preach*. Timothy made a natural candidate, for he was raised on the Scriptures and understood them thoroughly (2 Tim. 3:15). When Paul was forced out of Thessalonica and Berea, he left Timothy and Silas behind to finish the work that he started (Acts 17:14–15), having every confidence in them to complete the work. He trusted Titus to preach on Crete (Titus 1:5) and in Dalmatia (2 Tim. 4:10), Crescens he sent to Galatia (2 Tim. 4:10), and as a result of his time spent with Barnabas on the first mission tour, Barnabas was able to then replicate and expand Paul's evangelistic ministry when they separated (Acts 15:39–40). Even men like Urbanus (Rom. 16:9), Clement (Phil. 4:3), and Philemon (Phm. 1) are labeled with the affectionate term "fellow worker"—a term Paul only uses for those who are his partners in spreading the gospel.

Paul trained others to *teach* his converts. There isn't a big difference between preaching and teaching, but Paul didn't write letters to Priscilla and Aquila, or Tychicus teaching them how to "do the work of an evangelist" as he did Timothy (2 Tim. 4:5). Instead, Priscilla and Aquila were the kinds of people that Paul could entrust to host churches in their home (in both Rome and Ephesus: Rom. 16:3–5; 1 Cor. 16:19), giving systematic instruction in the Scriptures. They were competent in transmitting the intricacies of the faith to Apollos (Acts 18:26), who then became a powerful teacher himself before the Jews (Acts 18:28) and the Corinthians (1 Cor. 1:12, 3:6).

Even those who delivered Paul's letters to the churches were expected to be able to answer questions about the letter's intended meaning,[10] and for that reason Phoebe must be counted

---

10. Michael Gorman, *Apostle of the Crucified Lord: A Theological Introduction to Paul and His Letters* (Grand Rapids: Eerdmans, 2004), 87: "These cosenders or, more often, other associates would also deliver the mail and, following ancient custom, probably interpret its contents."

among those able to teach for Paul. That she was to be welcomed, or "received" by the Roman congregation (Rom. 16:1–2) strongly suggests that she is the one carrying the letter to them, and as the bearer of the letter would have been expected to answer any questions that arose about Paul's intentions. No one could have done so without a firm indoctrination into Paul's gospel and theology. The same can be said for Tychicus, who was a candidate alongside Artemas to deliver the letter to Titus on Crete (Titus 3:12).

By all indications, both within the letters themselves and from what we know of ancient letter-writing practices, Paul's normal practice was to use a scribe to write down the letters as he spoke them. Not everyone was suited for this, for only about fifteen percent of those in the ancient world could read and write. Paul used the literate around him to compose his letters. This was a natural method of discipleship, for who could script the book of Romans (as Tertius did: Rom. 16:22) without becoming familiar with Paul's gospel? Paul allowed men like Tertius, Sosthenes (1 Cor. 1:1), and Silas (1 Thess. 1:1; 2 Thess. 1:1; cf. also 1 Peter 5:12) a mention in his letters because he trusted them. Paul's most prolific author was Luke, who composed for Paul 2 Timothy (2 Tim. 4:11), Acts, and possibly had a hand in composing Colossians (4:14; though cf. 1:1), 1 Timothy, and Titus. The early church fathers suggest that Paul's preaching lay behind the Gospel of Luke,[11] hinting at Luke's familiarity with Paul's preaching of the life of Christ and perhaps also his role in scripting out Paul's dictated letters.[12]

---

11. Irenaeus, *Against Heresies*: "Luke also, the companion of Paul, recorded in a book the Gospel preached by him" [in The Ante-Nicene Fathers, eds. A. R. Roberts and J. Donaldson, vol 1 (Peabody, MA: 1999), 3.1.1]; Origen, *Commentary on Matthew*, [in Eusebius, *Church History*, 6.25.5]: "Next came that of Luke, who wrote for Gentile converts the gospel praised by Paul"; Eusebius, *Church History* 3.4.8: "And they say that Paul meant to refer to Luke's Gospel wherever, as if speaking of some gospel of his own, he used the words, 'according to my Gospel.'"

12. T. C. Skeat, "'Especially the Parchments': A Note on 2 Timothy 4:13," *Journal of Theological Studies* 30 (1979): 173-177, long ago noted that the pastoral Epistles bore evidence of dictation rather than careful, deliberate penmanship.

Preaching and teaching the gospel was Paul's missional vocation. Letter-writing allowed Paul to continue his teaching ministry when he couldn't be with his readers. Paul trained apprentices to assist him in this endeavor at every level and in so doing ensured that the gospel was communicated in ways that outreached and outlived Paul's influence.

You Win Some, You Lose Some

There were many in Paul's company who were loyal and devoted to him. But not even a successful discipler like Paul could ensure the faithfulness of all of his converts. In fact, some deserted Paul, proving that, like Jesus's own experience with Judas, some will leave, even betray. There was Demas, a "fellow worker" who accompanied Paul to Rome (Col. 4:14; Phm. 24), but who later deserted him (2 Tim. 4:10). There were Phygelus and Hermogenes, who left Paul during his second imprisonment (2 Tim. 1:15), and Hymenaeus, who Paul had hoped would repent (1 Tim. 1:20), but who eventually "wandered away from the truth" (2 Tim. 2:17–18). Their names now stand in the eternal record of Scripture as those who abandoned Paul, rejected his teaching and mentoring, and chose their own way. He considered their abandonment a repudiation of the way and teaching of Christ.

And then there's John Mark. If you have any familiarity with him at all, you recognize him as the one who abandoned Paul on his first missionary journey, and the man who caused such sharp disagreement between Paul and Barnabas as to part them. But there's a fuller story here—one that illustrates Paul's intensity about the gospel, his seriousness in discipling, and his tremendous grace and forgiveness (which is often absent from portraits of Paul).

John Mark was the issue that separated Paul and Barnabas—more specifically, Mark's abandoning[13] of the first mission in its

---

13. The word Luke uses here has a strong sense of "desert" or "withdraw from someone," not just going back home. See W. Bauer, W. F. Arndt, and F. Wilbur

early stages (Acts 13:13). Mark had previously been living in Jerusalem with his mother, Mary, allowing believers to gather in their
home to pray for Peter's release from prison (Acts 12:12). When
Paul and Barnabas took a love offering to Jerusalem to help with
famine relief (Acts 11:27–30), they brought Mark back from Jerusalem to Antioch (Acts 12:25). He accompanied them on their first
mission tour through the villages of Cyprus and on to the south
shores of Asia Minor, where for some reason he abandoned them.

The split between Paul and Mark seems irreconcilable in Luke's
initial recounting (Acts 15:36–41). Numerous theories have been
advanced as to Mark's exact reason for leaving. Proposed theories point to illness, to a growing homesickness and disgust with
itinerant ministry,[14] to fear and danger of banditry in the Pisidian
hillsides,[15] and to Mark's jealousy that Paul's leadership was outrun-
ning that of his cousin Barnabas. I am persuaded by Longenecker's
argument that John Mark, a Jew from Jerusalem, had trouble offering the gospel (as Paul understood it—without adherence to the
Mosaic traditions) to Gentiles.[16] Illness and "preaching somewhere
else" are inadequate to explain the sharp and bitter dispute that
arose between Paul and Barnabas over Mark's decision. An abandonment of the God-revealed gospel Paul preached seems to fit the
bill (cf. Gal. 1:6–12). That Luke recounts their disagreement on the
heels of the Jerusalem Council's decision regarding Gentile conformity to Jewish tradition also suggests that John Mark had trouble
accepting Gentile inclusion into the promises of Israel (or at least
the way Paul was going about it).

But there is more to the story, and if we are to get a true
glimpse of Paul's discipling efforts, we must come to understand

---

Gingrich, "*apochōreō*," *Greek-English Lexicon of the New Testament and Other Early
Christian Literature*, 2nd ed., 102.
14. F. F. Bruce, *The Pauline Circle* (Grand Rapids: Eerdmans, 1985), 18, 75.
15. J. W. McGarvey, *New Commentary on Acts of Apostles*, vol. 2, (1892. Reprint, Delight, AR: Gospel Light, n.d.), 11–12.
16. Longenecker, *The Ministry and Message of Paul* (Grand Rapids: Zondervan, 1971),
43, 59–61.

it. After their split, Mark accompanied Barnabas in visiting the very churches they had visited on their first journey. Sometime after this journey, Paul and Mark were reconciled, for he wound up with Paul in Rome. Writing from a Roman prison Paul told the church in Colossae that Mark, "the cousin of Barnabas," was with him, and that they were to welcome him (Col. 4:10). Nothing else is said at this point. One gets the impression that Paul is still very cautious. As Paul gave Mark's greetings to Philemon (from Rome) he referred to Mark as one of his "fellow workers" (Phm. 24).

Sometime between Acts 13 and Acts 28, Mark and Paul had been reconciled, for Mark had accompanied Paul to Rome and was helping him. Mark also spent time with Peter in Rome (1 Peter 5:13), and tradition says that he was writing down Peter's eyewitness account of the ministry of Jesus, now encapsulated in the Gospel of Mark.[17] By the time of Paul's second imprisonment, knowing his life was about to end, he asked for Timothy to bring Mark to see him, "because he is helpful to me in my ministry" (2 Tim. 4:11). In his last days, Paul sincerely wanted Mark at his side. Paul and John Mark had worked through their disagreements, and the restoration was part of the discipling process.

Discipling Like Paul

What is there left to say of those like Archippus (Phm. 2), Onesimus (Phm. 10–13; Col. 4:9), Syzygus (Phil. 4:3),[18] Stachys (Rom. 16:9), Persis (Rom. 16:12), Jason (Acts 17:5; Rom. 16:21), or any of those mentioned in the greetings of Paul's letters? Our discussion has only been cursory, and yet it remains clear that

---

17. Justin Martyr, *Dialogues* [in The Ante-Nicene Fathers, eds. A. R. Roberts and J. Donaldson, vol 1 (Peabody, MA: 1999), 106]; Irenaeus, *Against Heresies*, 3.1.2; Tertullian, *Against Marcion* 4.5; Clement of Alexandria, *Hypotyposes* (in Eusebius, *History of the Church* 6.14.5–7). Eusebius records the tradition of Papias that Mark wrote down what he heard Peter preach and teach (*History of the Church* 3.39.15). For a thorough analysis of this tradition see Richard Bauckham, *Jesus and the Eyewitnesses: The Gospels as Eyewitness Testimony* (Grand Rapids: Eerdmans, 2006), 12–38, 154–182

18. If this is indeed a person. The word means "yokefellow."

Paul was conscientious to train others to help him in his work. He was not content to make converts and leave them to grow on their own. He was always concerned to choose men and women worthy of the task for training in the teaching of the gospel, and trained them to represent him in his absence and, in some cases, to carry on evangelistic efforts of their own.

Paul's success in making disciples calls into question many of the practices (or nonexistent practices) of the modern North-American church. Many churches have no systematic plan for turning attenders into believers, believers into disciples, and disciples into co-workers and ministers. The biblical ideal is that *all* who come to faith participate in the ministry of the kingdom, rather than elevating a separate class to do the work of ministry for them (Exod. 19:6; Eph. 2:10; 1 Pet. 2:9; Rev. 5:10). Churches often approach discipleship in a programmatic fashion, creating cookie-cutter programs and classes aimed at the most widely-targeted audience. I write from experience about this, for of the churches I've been connected with in my ministry career, only one had a systematic plan for discipleship—I designed it, and it was exactly the cookie-cutter version I just described.

I see something quite different in Paul. While Paul's method was to preach the gospel to as wide an audience as possible, he regularly identified gifted and committed individuals for deeper personal training in the work of ministry. Paul was *always* looking to train someone. While some of the details of Paul's life are a bit sketchy, even absent from the written record, I am hard-pressed to find any time in Paul's Christian life when he wasn't training a disciple. Even on his journey to a Roman prison, several people accompanied him, and during his second imprisonment he was still encouraging Timothy and seeking the fellowship of Luke and Mark. His disciple-making efforts were intentional, continuous, and lifelong. And at the end, these people returned the favor by being a comfort to Paul.

How was he so successful? How did Paul take these men and turn them from religious Jews or pagans into committed ministers and co-workers for the kingdom? Very simply, time on task. I don't see in Paul a committed program, a systematic plan of discipleship. Rather, Paul's method of disciple-making amounted to having each apprentice spend time with him doing everything he did. (The kids these days call it "doing life together.") They traveled with him, listened to him preach, studied Scripture with him, transcribed his letters, and stood in his place when he was forced away. Sometimes they worked in the artisan shop with him, listening to him teach and evangelize those who were interested in the way of Jesus. Greg Ogden likens Paul's discipling efforts to spiritual parenting, and I would not wholly disagree.[19] Sometimes it involved teaching, at other times entrusting his "children" with doing the work under his supervision, and on a few occasions requiring discipline and correction. It always involved Paul bringing would-be apprentices to his side, and sharing with them the business of the gospel in everyday life. He offered them what my wife calls "an open invitation to participate in daily life and ministry."

Several years ago I began re-evaluating my ministry in this area. Johnson University Florida has a discipling group program that all students are required to participate in, and after serving in it for a few years, I began to re-evaluate my role in it. Because we continually have too few leaders for the student body, the groups are regularly large, which hinders deep-level relationship building. After processing some alternative ideas (and in large part, after reading Greg Ogden's *Transforming Discipleship*) I identified three young men on campus whom I invited to study with me for one year. We met weekly, shared concerns about our respective ministries, studied spirituality, memorized Scripture, and challenged one another. They understood from the first invitation (because I made it a condition for participation) that they would each, after one year, choose three men of their own on campus to invite to their own

---

19. Greg Ogden, *Transforming Discipleship* (Downers Grove, IL: InterVarsity Press, 2003), 99–118.

groups. Our weekly meetings were not enough to train them for the task, so we also met outside the confines of our weekly meeting. We ate together, we studied together in the classroom, and visited each other's homes when tragedy struck. This program is now in its seventh year. Those three young men have trained their own disciples, who are now carrying the work I began in that small group. My commitment to these young men was, in an effort to imitate Paul, to share life together in the hopes that they would see in me a pattern of life and ministry to be imitated.

If you're reading this and you find yourself woefully inadequate to train someone for kingdom life and ministry, I would encourage you to seek out someone who can become a mentor for you in Christian faith. It may be a minister, a teacher, a trusted Christian friend, or someone who you'd simply like to imitate. If you're looking for help in finding your own apprentices and "children" in the faith, I suggest Ogden's *Transforming Discipleship* and Anderson and Reese's *Spiritual Mentoring: A Guide for Seeking and Giving Direction* as excellent resources to begin with.

Thomas Tobin, writing of Paul's spirituality, claims that "no spirituality is timeless."[20] And yet I find Paul committing the things he said, did, and became to others, so that people could imitate him in their own time. He wouldn't have passed those things on to them if he didn't believe that the practices were relevant in every time and every culture. Further, he wouldn't have asked his followers to pass those things on to *their* disciples were the things not timeless. In training others for faith and kingdom ministry, Paul imitated his Lord and gave practical expression to the work the Spirit was doing in his life. This practical partnership with the Spirit in helping believers attain spiritual maturity is at the heart of authentic Christian spirituality.

---

20. Thomas H. Tobin, *The Spirituality of Paul* (Eugene, OR: Wipf and Stock, 1987), 42.

■

CHAPTER 5

"We Proclaim Christ":
Proclamation of the Gospel

■ PROP UP WHOMEVER YOU WANT from the ancient world: Herod the Great, who refurbished Solomon's temple and littered Judea with theaters and hippodromes; Alexander the Great, personal apprentice of Aristotle and the man who expanded the borders of Greece all the way to Persia; Augustus, who saved the empire from a century of civil war and whose birthday became the first day of the new calendar year[1]; Musonius Rufus, whose conservative approach gave the Stoics a lasting place among the world's ethical codes; the Flavian Dynasty (Vespasian, Titus, and Domitian), whose influence was so pervasive in Asia Minor that a system of worship—complete with high priest and choir—arose for nothing more than to sing their praises.[2] Prop up whomever you want. When it comes to raw influence, and the ability to change an entire empire in just a little less than two decades, Paul outranks them all.

In just a few short years, Paul had taken the message of the gospel beyond the borders of Judea into the Gentile areas of the Roman Empire. F. F. Bruce says that Paul "outstripped all others as a pioneer missionary and planter of churches, and nothing can detract from his achievement as the Gentiles' apostle *par excellence.*"[3]

---

1. Steven J. Friesen, *Imperial Cults and the Apocalypse of John* (Oxford: University Press, 2001), 32–36.
2. Ibid., 39–55, 104–121.
3. F. F. Bruce, *Paul: Apostle of the Heart Set Free*, 18.

Though Jesus was a Jewish Messiah, Paul saw in Jesus's death and resurrection hope for all the nations. The proclamation of the gospel was central for Paul's spirituality, for through the preaching of the gospel men and women placed faith in Christ and the power of Spirit was unleashed (Rom. 10:14–15; Gal. 3:1–2).

There are several ways that we could approach the subject of Paul's preaching as a function and tool of his spirituality. We could outline his preaching of the gospel across the Roman Empire, tracing his steps city by city. We could describe each of the places he preached in detail and examine how Paul's ministry fulfilled Jesus's desire that his disciples be his witnesses to the "ends of the earth" (Acts 1:8). It would also be appropriate to discuss how Paul's preaching effected conversion among his hearers, noting whether they responded out of faith or were predestined by God for eternal life. We could debate whether he preached to the poorer people or among the more aristocratic strata of Hellenistic society. These are matters of history, theology, and exegesis. Our approach is more broad, and will attempt to paint an overall picture against which we can silhouette kingdom life in the twenty-first century. So here's where we're headed: We'll examine Paul's calling as an apostle to the Gentiles, set out the basic parameters of his message, and then see how he fleshed out that same basic message for different groups (Jews and Gentiles). This should give us some clue as to what preaching the gospel means in our day and how we are to go about it.

Paul, Apostle to the Gentiles

Paul's ministry of evangelism sprang from his call to be an "apostle of Christ Jesus."[4] Over and again in the Old Testament

---

4. Paul specifically identifies himself as an "apostle of Christ Jesus" in 1 Cor. 1:1; 2 Cor. 1:1; Eph. 1:1; Col. 1:1; 1 Tim. 1:1; 2 Tim. 1:1; Titus 1:1. He refers to himself as an "apostle" (with no qualifiers) in Rom. 1:1, 11:13; 1 Cor. 4:9, 9:1-2, 15:9; 2 Cor. 11:5, 12:11; Gal. 1:1, 17; 1 Thess. 2:6; 1 Tim. 2:7; 2 Tim. 1:11.

God sent prophets to speak his message to his people.[5] When Jesus came on the scene, he continually spoke of being "sent" by his Father in the tradition of the Old Testament prophets. Jesus was God's "apostle" (lit. "one sent"), and the cognate terms for "sent" appear in references to Jesus frequently in the Gospels.[6]

Some were designated "apostles" because they were eyewitnesses to the resurrected Christ and commissioned personally by him to spread the message of his resurrection. This is the main qualification asserted by both Peter (Acts 1:21–22) and Paul (1 Cor. 9:1). This would include not only the original Twelve (minus Judas, plus Matthias), but also Paul, and perhaps James the brother of Jesus (Gal. 1:19). Of these, Paul was "untimely born" (1 Cor. 15:8 NASB), and considered himself the last of the eyewitnesses to be set apart for proclamation and protection of the gospel message (1 Cor. 15:8). If Paul really was the "last" of the apostles, then there is no succession of eyewitnesses bearing apostolic authority beyond their lifetime.

The basic meaning of the term "apostle," though, is simply "one who is sent," one who stands in for another, or one who bears a message in another's stead. In this sense, Paul and Barnabas were "sent" from the Jerusalem Council to deliver the resulting letter to the churches (Acts 15:22–23), and they are together called "apostles" by Luke (Acts 14:4). Paul's apostleship was absolutely tied to his Damascus road experience of the risen Jesus, and it was this aspect of apostleship that he hung his hat on. Paul was seriously challenged by some "super-apostles" in Corinth who were questioning his right to call himself an apostle. Perhaps they

---

5. The cognate Hebrew word for "sent" appears in the Old Testament more than 800 times. Of those, God is the subject more than 200 times. And of those, the Septuagint (Greek translation of the Hebrew Old Testament) uses the word *apostellō* seventy-five percent of the time. See Walter C. Kaiser, Jr., *Mission in the Old Testament: Israel as a Light to the Nations* (Grand Rapids: Baker, 2000), 11–12. The most frequent sending is that of God sending a prophet.

6. See C. G. Kruse, "Apostle," in *Dictionary of Jesus and the Gospels*, eds. Joel B. Green, Scot McKnight, and I. Howard Marshall (Downers Grove, IL: InterVarsity Press, 1992), 29–30.

acknowledged his claim to be an "apostle," but only as one sent from the Jerusalem apostles and not as one who had ultimate authority in the church. Paul pointed out to them (and to the Galatians, where he also faced this challenge) that willingness to suffer on behalf of Christ was the mark of a true apostle, and on those grounds, he had them beat (2 Cor. 11:16–29, Gal. 6:17).[7]

Wrapped up with his call to be an apostle is certainly the statement that God "set [him] apart from birth" (Gal. 1:15) to be an apostle to the Gentiles. One has to wonder whether if God had decided beforehand that Paul would be his apostle, did he not also foreordain Paul's persecution of the church? This leads to difficult questions about divine sovereignty and free will, and we're no closer to an answer on that issue than we were in the times of Augustine or Calvin. But rather than thinking of it in post-Reformation American evangelical terms, consider Paul's statement against comments made by Isaiah and Jeremiah that echo this exact same language. Isaiah spoke of the Servant of the Lord as being set apart from birth to reconcile Israel to God and then become "a light for the Gentiles" (Isa. 49:1, 5–6). In a similar fashion, Jeremiah writes that he too had been set apart from birth for the express purpose of being a "prophet to the nations," or Gentiles (Jer. 1:5). Inherent in the call of both Jeremiah and Isaiah was a belief that God set them apart from birth to bring his salvation to the Gentiles. This is exactly how Paul sees his own ministry: God set him apart from birth so that he might preach the gospel among the Gentiles (Gal. 1:15–16). His comment has less to do with the foreordained will of God and more to do with

---

7. It seems that the false teachers in both Galatia and Corinth shared similarities in their Jewish-Christian backgrounds. The consensus seems to be that they were demanding that Gentiles participate in circumcision, Sabbath-keeping, and Jewish food purity in order to avoid opposition and persecution by Jewish non-believers. Paul counted suffering at the hands of the peoples' own countrymen (1 Thess 2:14–15) in the same tradition of Jesus, who faced the same opposition among the Jewish leadership for not scrupulously observing these laws. See Barrett, *Paul: An Introduction to His Thought*, 22–39.

Paul interpreting his own ministry against the calls of the two great Old Testament prophets who foretold the offer of salvation to the Gentiles that Paul was preaching.[8]

The Gospel Paul Preached

Paul was an emissary for Christ, an ambassador who made Christ and his will known among the Gentiles. But what was the message? In *The Spirituality of Jesus* I suggested that Jesus's preaching of the kingdom of God included aspects of "justice, mercy, and righteousness" (Micah 6:8; Mt. 23:23). But Paul rarely spoke of the kingdom of God, at least not in the way that Jesus did. Of course, Paul's letters are fruitful with kingdom ideas,[9] but as we peruse the book of Acts we don't find him preaching Jesus's message that "the kingdom of God has drawn near" (Mk. 1:15; Lk. 10:9, 11; 21:31).

Many see Paul's preaching as the basic proclamation of Christ crucified. Indeed, Paul admits this himself—"we preach Christ crucified" (1 Cor. 1:23)—and the language of crucifixion is prominent in his speaking and writing, so much so that Michael Gorman speaks of Paul's ministry as one of "cruciformity."[10]

---

8. Andreas Köstenberger and Peter O'Brien, *Salvation to the Ends of the Earth: A Biblical Theology of Mission*, New Studies in Biblical Theology, ed. D. A. Carson (Downers Grove, IL: InterVarsity Press, 2001), 165–166.

9. In *The Spirituality of Jesus*, 151–154, I defined the essence of the kingdom as mercy, justice, and loving-kindness (Micah 6:8; Mt. 23:23). Paul expressed many of these same ideas in his letters. For example, Paul is the object of God's mercy (1 Cor. 7:25; 1 Tim. 1:13, 16) and characterizes God as merciful throughout his letters (Rom. 9:16, 18, 23, 11:30–32, 12:1, 15:9; 2 Cor. 4:1; Eph. 2:4; Phil. 2:27; 2 Tim. 1:16, 18; Titus 3:5). Paul's emphasis of the "righteousness of God" in Romans has strong linguistic ties with the righteousness of God revealed in Isaiah, which is coupled with the offer of God's salvation (Isa. 42:6–7, 21–22, 45:8, 13, 46:13, 51:5–8, 56:1, 59:16–17, 61:10, 62:1). The "loving-kindness" works out into brotherly love for Paul, which he constantly reminds his readers to practice (Rom. 13:8–10; 1 Cor. 13:1–14:1; Gal. 5:14–15; 1 Thess. 4:9–10).

10. Michael Gorman, *Cruciformity: Paul's Narrative Spirituality of the Cross* (Grand Rapids: Eerdmans, 2001), 18: "In Paul's experience, God's will and person are known through the cross of Jesus the Messiah and Lord. In other words, cruciformity is the character of God."

But Paul's message of Jesus's crucifixion was simply a prelude to the message that he wanted to preach to both Jew and Gentile: that Jesus is now enthroned at God's right hand as Lord of the universe. The proof is in the resurrection. Of course, in order to tell the story of Jesus's resurrection, Paul first needed to tell the story of how Jesus died—on a Roman cross, scourge of the empire and cursed in the eyes of the Jews (Deut. 21:23; 1 Cor. 1:23). If he was hanged on a "tree," then he was cursed. But if he was raised from the dead, it was proof that the curse had been lifted (or absent all along) and that he was innocent of all charges. That God raised him from the dead *proves* his innocence. If he was innocent of the charges and went willingly to his death, then he suffered vicariously for the atonement of the world. Paul outlined this basic message in Philippians 2:5-12:[11] Jesus willingly left his high place in heaven, became obedient unto death, and as a result of his obedience, God vindicated him and gave him his own name, that of "Lord."[12]

In fact, this is how the earliest (Jewish) Christians came to speak of Jesus, in terms that echo the name of God. Among the earliest Jewish believers the term "Lord" (Gk. *kurios*) was the preferred substitute for God's name, Yahweh. When the Old Testament was translated into Greek (commonly called the Septuagint), "Lord" was the term used to translate the name of God

---

11. One of the serious questions about the hymn is whether Paul composed it expressly for this letter or adopted it from a well-known Christian hymn. Among the many who believe that Paul did not compose it are Gorman, *Cruciformity*, 88-92; and Barrett, *Paul: An Introduction to His Thought*, 105-109. N. T. Wright, *The Climax of the Covenant: Christ and the Law in Pauline Theology* (Minneapolis: Fortress, 1993), 98, believes that the hymn is so in line with themes running through the entire corpus of Philippians that it only makes sense that Paul composed it for this purpose: "the passage fits its present context so well that it is very hard to see it in any way as a detached, or even detachable, hymn about Christ."

12. The Christ-hymn of Philippians 2:5-12 strongly echoes the text of Isaiah 45:23-24, where every knee bows and every tongue confesses that Yahweh is Lord and finds salvation in Him. That Paul puts this language about God in the poem as a reference to Jesus further indicates that, in Paul's mind, Jesus was Lord of the universe, seated at the right hand of the Father.

(Yahweh). It was also the term that the earliest Jewish believers used to speak of Jesus. They believed that Jesus was enthroned as Lord of heaven and earth, seated at God's right hand. Their belief wasn't concocted from their own desires, but was formed from and completely commensurate with Old Testament themes of the Son of David (who, like David, will be enthroned as God's "son"; cf. Ps. 2; Acts 2:25-26) and the "son of man" (who is enthroned at God's right hand in the midst of suffering; cf. Dan. 7:13-14).[13] The earliest Christians saw Jesus enthroned at the Father's right hand, having been vindicated in resurrection. They believed him to be the "Lord," and this is Paul's basic message.

If he is Lord, then he is Lord of the *entire world*, not just the Jews. The Old Testament often speaks of God's salvation going out beyond the borders of Israel and welcoming in the Gentiles. Bringing Jews and Gentiles together in the ancient world was bound to cause problems, and Paul used his knowledge of the Old Testament to demonstrate to Jews and Gentiles alike that the God of the Jews had been working from the beginning to bring them together and build a people for himself comprised not of bloodlines (though it came through the Jews) but of faith. We might have thought that Paul's favorite proof texts would come from Isaiah, for the Song of the Suffering Servant is rich with themes hinting that God's salvation would be extended through the Servant to the Gentiles.[14] But Paul's most favored text for proving God's plan to include Jews and Gentiles in the same family came from the Law. Ingenious (and ironic!) when you think about it: Paul, a Jew, used the Torah (which gave laws to separate

---

13. For more on how these themes of suffering and enthronement are developed in the "Son of man" motif in both Daniel and the Gospels, see L. Hardin, "Son of Man," in *The Lexham Bible Dictionary*, eds. J. D. Barry and L. Wentz (Bellingham, WA: Lexham Press, 2012).

14. Gentiles are co-heirs with Israel of Yahweh's salvation in Isaiah 42:1; 49:1, 5-6, 22; 51:5; 52:10, 15; 56:3-8; 60:9, 11; 61:11.

Jews from the rest of the world) to prove that Gentiles are co-heirs with Jews of God's promises.

The preferred text is the promise to Abraham, given long before the Law ever existed, that "through your offspring all nations on earth will be blessed" (Gen. 12:3, 18:18, 22:18, 26:4, 28:14). Paul invoked Abraham's trust in God about the promised birth of his son Isaac (Gen. 15:5; cf. Rom. 4:1-25, Gal. 3:6-9) as an example of what true faith in God looks like: He "believed God, and it was credited to him as righteousness" (Gal. 3:6; cf. Rom. 4:3, 22-23). As a result, God rewarded Abraham and promised him that he would be the father of "all nations" (Gen. 22:18), not just the Jewish nation. Paul picked up on the Abrahamic promise and preached to Jew and Gentile alike that "all nations will be blessed" through the seed of Isaac. Isaac was the beginning of the bloodline of the Jews, and through the Jewish bloodlines came Jesus, who is, in type, *the Seed* of Isaac (Gal. 3:16, 19). Some Jewish believers naturally objected that, because the Abrahamic covenant was sealed with circumcision, Gentiles ought to also be circumcised to participate in the promise of Messiah's salvation (cf. Gal. 5:2-6, 6:12-16). Paul was quick to remind his Jewish compatriots that Abraham was declared righteous by his faith, long before he was ever circumcised (Rom. 4:10; Gal. 3:6-9).

This was Paul's message: Jesus is Lord of the universe, crowned so in his resurrection. He is the Seed of Abraham that unites the world. The salvation that he brings is universal, including both Jews and Gentiles, and Paul preached it to both groups. It came off differently to each group, and not always in ways that were kosher or civically responsible.

Preaching to the Religious Establishment

Wherever Paul went, he always began his preaching in the synagogue. Jesus was fond of Gentiles, and praised them when they demonstrated more faith in him than his own people (Mt. 8:10-12). But when he trained his own disciples to preach in the towns and backwater burgs of Galilee, he instructed them *not* to preach among the Gentiles, or even the Samaritans, but to focus exclusively on the Jews (Mt. 10:5–6). By instructing his disciples this way, he kept in front of them that "salvation is from the Jews" (Jn. 4:22). The Gentiles would be blessed, to be sure, but they would be blessed through the Jewish Messiah, and it was only fair and right that the Jews got first dibs.

So Paul began in the synagogues. When he went to Cyprus, Pisidian Antioch, and Iconium, he began in the synagogues. When he went to Philippi, he went down to the river where there was a synagogue and preached there (Acts 16:13). Luke describes Paul beginning in the synagogue in nearly every city he visited thereafter, from Thessalonica, to Berea, to Athens, Corinth, and Ephesus. Everywhere he went, Paul began his evangelistic ministry in the worship services and gathering places of his own countrymen.

What did he preach there? That Jesus is Lord and is seated at the right hand of God. Of course, for Paul this came as a result of Jesus's resurrection from the dead. So for his Jewish audience, Paul had to begin with the message of a *suffering* messiah. His synagogue message is summarized for us in Acts 17 as Paul began his ministry in Thessalonica. Luke tells us that he went to the synagogue and preached that it was necessary that the Messiah suffer and *then* enter his glory (Acts 17:3). Most Jews believed that the Messiah would be enthroned in glory, but the understanding of exactly what kind of glory and how it would happen varied among Jews of the first century. One element seems pervasive, though: In line with the promise that the Messiah would be the Son of David (2 Sam. 7:11–16), and because David ran the neighboring nations from Israel at the tip of the sword, many believed that the Messiah would purge Israel of its Gentile elements and purify the nation by steel.[15]

---

15. The most famous passage is the Psalm of Solomon 17, where after praise for God's election of David to the throne of Israel, the psalmist anticipates "the son of David" (Ps. Sol. 17:21), also known as "the Lord Messiah" (17:32), coming to set Israel to rights again by first destroying the Gentile rulers around him (17:22–25). Only after

But Paul's message was that of a *suffering* messiah, now exalted. "He humbled himself by becoming obedient to death . . . therefore God exalted him to the highest place" (Phil. 2:8-9). This is exactly the message that Jesus taught his disciples: "Did not the Christ have to suffer these things and then enter his glory?" (Lk. 24:26; cf. Mt. 16:21, Lk. 18:31-33, 24:7, 46-47). Central for Paul was the belief that Jesus suffered, rose from the dead in bodily form (1 Cor. 15:20-21), and is now seated at God's right hand.

Paul was successful evangelizing in the synagogue. How could he not be, knowing Judaism and her Scriptures so intimately? In Thessalonica he won over some prominent Jews (Acts 17:4). He was successful evangelizing Jews in Ephesus, Rome, Paphos, Pisidian Antioch, Iconium, Lystra, Derbe, Philippi, Berea, Athens, and Corinth. And when he finally made it to Jerusalem at the end of Acts, the testimony that preceded him was that thousands of Jews had come to believe in Jesus because of Paul's ministry (Acts 21:20).

It's hard to hear Paul's message to the religious establishment afresh in our Jesus-saturated culture. While the world seems hostile to the message we preach, it's not from ignorance of the basic facts of Jesus's life. Many non-believers understand that Jesus preached a message of radical love and was crucified, and they generally hold him in high regard. Their hostility stems more from the church's hypocrisy in living out the message, and from misunderstanding what Jesus was *really* about.

The church can be just as mired in misconception about the person and life of Jesus as the average non-believer. Because of my connection with Johnson University Florida, I'm on the road about thirty weekends a year, filling the pulpit for absent preachers, representing the college, and speaking at a few events. Most people connected with Johnson University Florida know that my primary work is in New Testament studies, and primarily the life of Christ.

Israel has been cleansed of Gentiles will he re-establish the tribal allotments of land and rule Israel in righteousness (17:26-32).

So if churches give me a wide topical berth, I'll usually preach from the Gospels. One of the things I've noticed in the past several years is that the portrait of Jesus assumed in most churches is in some ways out of alignment with the Jesus portrayed in Scripture. Of course, I tread carefully. I don't go from church to church challenging the "traditions of the elders." That was Jesus's job, and I would be ill-advised to usurp his place. But I do try, gently and with humility, to cast a picture of Jesus that is commensurate with Scripture and point out where our misalignment needs adjusting.

One of the things that seems pervasive in the collection of churches I spend the most time with is the idea that worship of Jesus is tied to political ideology. Every election year churches engage in culture wars, casting their approval for one candidate as godly and the other as evil. It exists on both sides of the political fence. I think Philip Yancey is right when he says of Jesus, "I have difficulty imagining him pondering whether Tiberius, Octavius, or Julius Caesar was 'God's man' for the empire. The politics of Rome were virtually irrelevant to the kingdom of God."[16] Jesus was not a right-wing Republican do-gooder who offered salvation to those who supported the troops and showed high levels of personal responsibility. But neither was he a left-wing Democratic social activist who offered civil rights in the name of the gospel. In Paul's preaching, he was God's Messiah, offering God's salvation to God's people. And he did so through his death and resurrection.

Preaching in the Public Square

Paul's preaching wasn't confined to the synagogue. Paul was the apostle to the Gentiles, and while his typical *modus operandi* was to start in the synagogue ("first for the Jew"), he quickly moved to the public arena ("then for the Gentile"; Rom. 1:16, 2:9–10). His message in both the synagogue and the public arena was the same:

---

16. Philip Yancey, *The Jesus I Never Knew* (Grand Rapids: Zondervan, 1995), 250.

Jesus, by his resurrection, is enthroned as the Lord of the universe. For the Jew, this meant a clear exposition from the prophets of the necessity of his suffering. For the Gentile, though, the basic message—Jesus is Lord—took a whole different approach.[17]

To most of us "the Lord" is another way of saying "God." We are to love the Lord with all our heart, mind, soul, and strength (Deut. 6:4–5; Mk. 12:29–30). Some of us may understand it against its medieval backgrounds, where the lord was someone who had superior social standing, and ruled as master over his slaves. The word is sometimes used this way in the New Testament. Jesus used the term *kurios* ("lord" or "master") to denote the landowner in some of the parables (Mt. 24:45–51, 25:14–30; Lk. 12:35–40, 42–48, 14:21–23, 16:1–8, 19:12–27), and assured his hearers that not everyone who addresses him by the title *kurios* would participate in the fullest expression of the kingdom (Mt. 7:21–23). But in the first century the term *kurios* was primarily the term loyal subjects of the Roman Empire used to refer to its ruler: Caesar.

Worship of the Roman emperor was growing in the first century, and fast! Emperors from the time of Augustus (who divinized his adopted father, Julius[18]), to Caligula (who divinized his horse), to the Flavian dynasty (Vespasian, Titus, and Domitian) had been proclaimed or hailed themselves as divine. Rome brought peace and safety to the world, established justice, and hailed the emperor as the one who brought it. When Roman historians wrote about it, and when Rome spread the propaganda, the favored

---

17. Larry Hurtado, *Lord Jesus Christ: Devotion to Jesus in Earliest Christianity* (Grand Rapids: Eerdmans, 2003), 111, suggests that Paul used the term *kurios* because it had meaning for both Jewish and Gentile audiences. For the Jew, the term *kurios* was the preferred translation of the Tetragrammaton (YHWH) in the Greek translation of the Old Testament. To Gentiles, it brought the connotation of one vastly superior, and therefore worked for both Jewish and Gentile audiences, but in a way that brought them together under one creed.

18. Shortly after his rule began, Augustus minted coins with his image on one side and the image of Julius on the other. The inscription on the coin read, "*Divus Iulius,*" translated "Son of the Divine Julius."

terms were "salvation," "savior," "justice/righteousness," and "good news," all in the name of the emperor who was "son of god."[19] So pervasive was the problem that by the time John wrote Revelation, the worship of the emperor had become one of the major issues confronting the church.[20]

If these assessments are accurate, then Paul's message to the Gentiles had the ring of "Jesus is Lord of the universe, not Caesar." What Rome promised to bring to the world—"salvation," "peace," and "prosperity" (or should I say, "life, liberty, and the pursuit of happiness"?)—was a sham and an empty promise. For Paul these things were only truly available in Jesus. So he went to the Areopagus, where the philosophers sat and discussed their ideas, and revealed to them that this "unknown god" they worshiped was actually Yahweh, and that his son was Lord of the universe, set to judge the world in his power (Acts 17:22–31). In Thessalonica Paul was run out of town for preaching "another king, one called Jesus" (Acts 17:7). And in the fiercely pro-Roman city of Philippi, Paul hailed Jesus as the *kurios* to whom every knee will bow and every tongue confess allegiance (Phil. 2:10–11). It's easy to see how Paul's message was counter-imperial. What's hard to see sometimes is that Paul's message was not primarily directed against the empire. Pick up the literature on Paul and the Roman Empire and you're bound to get the impression that Paul intentionally couched the message of the gospel so that it would run afoul of Caesar and cult. You almost get the impression from the printed works in this field that Paul had a beef with the Roman Empire and that the gospel of Jesus provided him with an opportunistic

---

19. See Warren Carter, *The Roman Empire and the New Testament: An Essential Guide* (Nashville: Abingdon Press, 2006), 83–92; N. T. Wright, *Paul: In Fresh Perspective* (Minneapolis: Fortress, 2005), 59–79; D. Georgi, "God Turned Upside Down," in *Paul and Empire: Religion and Power in Roman Imperial Society*, ed. Richard A. Horsley (Harrisburg, PA: Trinity Press International, 1997), 148–157; G. A. Deissmann, *Light from the Ancient East: The New Testament Illustrated by Recently Discovered Texts of the Graeco-Roman World*, trans. Lionel R. M. Strachan (Peabody, MA: Hendrickson, [1927] 1955), 338–378.

20. Friesen, *Imperial Cults*, 135–151.

tool with which to challenge the power structures inherent within the Roman system. I don't think that Paul had a problem with the Roman emperor, and I don't think that his gospel is more about taking down Rome rather than building God's kingdom.

Paul had no interest in seeing the empire destroyed. After all, it maintained justice in the world (Caesar "does not bear the sword for nothing," Rom. 13:4), developed a complex system of roads that made travel easy for Paul, and provided him certain rights and protections as a citizen. Paul's rhetoric originated in his unwavering belief that, because of his resurrection from the dead, Jesus is enthroned at the right hand of the Almighty God, and neither the emperor nor the would-be "gods" and idols so prominent in Hellenistic culture deserved to share the throne with him.

I've often wondered what it would take in modern America to preach a gospel commensurate with Paul's approach. As I said, Paul's message didn't stem from hatred of the empire. After all, he was a Roman citizen, and was willing to use that citizenship to his advantage (Acts 16:37-39; Acts 25:10-11). His message originated from the death, resurrection, and enthronement of Jesus, and Paul was willing to challenge anyone or anything who claimed to have the same kind of authority—either on earth or in heaven—that Jesus had by virtue of his resurrection. Does it mean that I preach a gospel of "Jesus is the leader of the free world, and the president isn't"? Perhaps. But most people don't worship the president of the United States. More subtle and pervasive (and very much in line with first-century emperor-worship) is the tendency of religious types in America to mix the worship of Jesus with adoration of America. Every July Fourth weekend, churches are filled with songs that exalt America and the freedom that God has bestowed to the world through her. Many don't realize that this is exactly the kind of thing that took place in the Roman Empire in the cult of Caesar. Don't get me wrong, reader. I love living here. Freedom is a wonderful thing. But I'm nervous about having the American flag on stage next to the cross. I'm nervous about exalting the glory of America alongside the glory of Christ. I'm nervous about singing patriotic worship songs in the assembly of Christ on national holidays. Most uncomfortable for me was the day we sang about returning to the heart of worship while the American flag was draped behind the lyrics on the screen. To mix the worship of Jesus with that of the empire would have been offensive to Paul. Jesus, by virtue of his resurrection, is exalted as Lord of the universe and shares power with no one.

It works itself out in other areas as well and in ways that challenge what we truly have come to respect and hold dear. If Jesus is enthroned as Lord, then he does not share power with Caesar. Or Darwin. Or Nietzsche. Or the President. Or the University. Or Hollywood. Or Consciousness. Or my cultural background. Or fame and success. Or even myself. Paul was so committed to Jesus's lordship that *nothing*–earthly, spiritual, or intellectual–could compete.

I think that's how we're to approach it still. The gospel is always running afoul of human power structures, philosophies, and ideologies. Our job is not to anger the local or federal authorities with our preaching of the gospel. That inevitably may happen, and we must be prepared to deal with it and endure it. *But it's not our primary responsibility.* Rather, our job is to preach the gospel of Jesus's lordship over every other thing. And if it causes us to run afoul of the government or the academy or popular cultural ideas, then let us be found faithful.

"Preaching the Gospel" and Christian Maturity

Paul's intention was to cover the empire with his evangelistic endeavors, preaching the gospel to Gentiles. In evangelical circles, "preaching the gospel" often refers to the telling of the death and resurrection of Jesus (with an accompanying invitation to accept his offer of eternal life), and certainly Paul meant to extend the invitation to as many as possible (1 Cor. 9:19). But there is evidence that "preaching the gospel" meant so much more to Paul than simply reciting the facts of Jesus's death and resurrection.

In the passage just mentioned (1 Cor. 9:19–23) Paul refers to his desire to "win" as many converts as possible. Köstenberger and O'Brien note,

> Although the verb to "win" has been taken to refer to Paul's goal of *converting* "as many as possible" (v. 19), including Jews and Gentiles (vv. 20-21), it cannot refer only to their conversion, since in verse 22 he speaks of his aim of winning "the weak," a designation which should be understood of Christians (rather than non-Christians; cf. Rom. 5:6) whose consciences trouble them about matters which are not in themselves wrong (cf. 1 Cor. 8).[21]

For Paul, evangelism was about making disciples, not just winning converts. His goal was to present them to Christ mature and complete at his return (Col. 1:28). The same ideas can be found in Paul's letter to the Romans. Paul had never visited the church in Rome (Rom. 1:10, 15:23), and longed to "preach the gospel" to them (Rom. 1:15). He was writing to a church already comprised of believers in Christ, so preaching the gospel meant more than the simple recitation of Jesus's trial and vindication. It included, for Paul, teaching the precepts of the faith in order to lead his converts into maturity.[22]

In this Paul takes his cue from Jesus, specifically from the Great Commission. Many English translations render the verbs in Matthew 28:19-20 as commands. "Go ye therefore" is the translation that I learned in my youth. But Jesus only offered one imperative, one command in the Great Commission, and it was to "make disciples" (Mt. 28:19; Gk. *mathēteusate*). The other verbs included there are participles, and indicate *how* the task of making disciples was to be completed (by going into the world, by baptizing them, and

---

21. Köstenberger and O'Brien, *Salvation to the Ends of the Earth*, 181.
22. Ibid., 181-183.

by teaching them to obey Jesus's commands). Some will hasten to point out to me that this is an oversimplification of the complexity of the Greek text, that sometimes participles can have "imperatival force" (i.e., "maybe he did mean 'Go' and '*make disciples*,' and '*baptize*' and '*teach*'").[23] But the most simple understanding of Jesus's language—to make disciples by going, baptizing, and teaching—seems to be how Paul understood his own evangelistic endeavors. He did not stay in Judea, but went into the outermost parts of the Roman Empire. He baptized his converts (or assumed that if they were believers, that they had already been baptized; cf. Rom. 6:3-4; 1 Cor. 1:13-17; Col. 2:12). His *modus operandi* was to stay in one place long enough to convey the teaching of the Christian faith and lifestyle, not just proclaim the death of Jesus in the marketplace and move on. He stayed in Ephesus three years and in Corinth for eighteen months. In some places (e.g., Thessalonica, Berea, Athens) Paul was not able to stay as long as he would have liked. But where he found a general receptivity to the Christian message which led to conversions, he did his best to stay and teach them the foundational elements of the Christian faith, and the Scriptural support for the Gentiles' inclusion into the promises of Israel's salvation.

Preaching the gospel is not simply about saying the words "Jesus died for your sins; will you accept him as your Savior?" Those words need to be said, but there is more to the preaching of the gospel. I see it on a regular basis here on campus. I teach in a four-year undergraduate Bible college. We train people for ministry, and many students come here with a profound and intense desire to do what God wants of them and to help spread the message of the gospel. But because the church in North America has generally become more and more biblically illiterate, the work of "preaching the gospel" takes place here every day. Many students come here with a general knowledge

---

23. Eckhard Schnabel, *Early Christian Mission*, 2 vols. (Downers Grove, IL: InterVarsity Press, 2004), 1:355-361, claims that the participle "going" is "either implicitly imperatival" or serves as the condition by which the "making disciples" happens, with "baptizing" and "teaching" part of the after-work of disciple-making.

that Jesus died for their sins, and I in no way suggest that they aren't believers by knowing only this. But every semester we baptize a small handful of students who have encountered the fullness of the gospel message for the first time. One student told me, after two semesters of Life of Christ, "Given the church environment I was raised in, I came to JUFL conditioned by a shallow, emotion-based perspective of Christianity, in which spiritual maturity was demonstrated by always being 'nice.'" The Christian faith is so much more, and it's time that churches begin, in Pauline fashion, to "preach the gospel."

∎

CHAPTER 6

"When You Come Together": Corporate Worship

∎ WE'VE GROWN ACCUSTOMED TO DEFINING "worship" in several different ways. Sometimes we use it to define the ceremonial aspects of the gathering of the church. Worship in this sense is what happens during the service, or "the worship service." Other times it is defined more narrowly as the musical portion of the service—there is the "worship," and then the sermon. In some circles the term "worship" is used to define a particular kind of song, as if "worship" songs were more reverential and God-honoring than hymns, chants, or choruses.

The testimony of Scripture reveals a more diverse canvas of vocabulary upon which the portrait of worship is painted. The authors of Scripture are consistent in their testimony that "worship" is only partly defined in ceremonial terms. The ceremonial elements are certainly there. The worship in the tabernacle (and later the temple) was ordered and ceremonious, with strict guidelines given by God on how worship ceremonies were to honor him (Lev. 1–7; 16; 23). When the Samaritan woman questioned Jesus about whether pure worship took place on Mount Gerizim or Mount Zion (in the Jerusalem temple, Jn. 4:19–20), she had ceremony in mind. When Jews went to worship, they went to participate in a worship *service*.

But worship also takes place *outside* the service, and the biblical writers continually point in this direction also. Abraham told his servants that he and Isaac were going up Mount Moriah to "worship," which for him consisted in offering up Isaac as a sacrifice (Gen. 22:5). Worship for Abraham, in that instance, consisted mainly of *obedience*. The first mention of the term "worship" in the New Testament appears on the lips of the Magi, who honored Jesus by presenting him with expensive gifts (Mt. 2:2, 11). Worship of foreign gods in the Old Testament is often defined as *devotion to* those gods, as lifestyle (Exod. 20:5; Num. 25:1–3, 5; Deut. 4:3–4; 2 Kings 17:34–39). Worship includes much more than ceremony, and Paul understood this. He invoked the image of temple sacrifice when he called us to offer our lives "as living sacrifices, holy and pleasing to God," which he calls our "spiritual act of worship" (Rom. 12:1). But he also thought of his entire life as an offering of worship to Christ (2 Tim. 4:6; Phil. 2:17), and expected his readers to do the same.

While worship is more broadly defined as encompassing all of life, in this chapter we focus on Paul's practice of attending worship *services*, of participating in the gathering of the community of God's people in ceremonial homage to God and to Christ. Just like his Master, Paul could regularly be found spending time with God's people in the corporate worship service at the appointed time for gathering. It was more than a gathering of individuals interested in Jesus. It was the time the Spirit became intimately present with his people, the time God's people honored him together and the church received edification and instruction from God and his Word.

Paul at Worship with the Church

In his Christian life, Paul regularly gathered with other believers for worship. Luke never comes out and says directly that Paul "went to church" or "attended the Christian worship service," but he portrays Paul preaching and teaching in a number of corporate worship settings. When Paul first came to Antioch with Barnabas, he "met with the church" for an entire year, preaching and teaching his gospel (Acts 11:25–26). After recruiting Timothy to join him, Paul took him through the towns in Galatia that he had previously visited, strengthening the churches, and the most con-

venient place to do this was in the weekly gathering of the churches (Acts 16:4–5). On one occasion Luke explicitly mentions that
Paul and the believers in Troas met "on the first day of the week,"
specifically "to break bread" (i.e., observe the Lord's Supper; Acts
20:7). In fact, it was in the midst of a Christian worship service,
"while they were worshiping the Lord and fasting," that the Holy
Spirit set Paul apart for mission work (Acts 13:2).

Anatomy of a First-Century Gathering

When Paul "went to church," he didn't go to an ornately
decorated building. The church didn't get in the business of buy-
ing property and erecting buildings for worship until about two
hundred years after the time of the apostles. Before that time,
the "church" in a particular city was comprised of one or more
house churches.[1] Believers like Priscilla and Aquila (Rom. 16:3–5;
1 Cor. 16:19), Nympha (Col. 4:15), Philemon (Phm. 2), Lydia
(Acts 16:40), and Gaius (Rom. 16:23) all hosted churches in
their homes. The service sometimes began with a meal (which in
Corinth degenerated into divisiveness), but this practice seems to
have passed away, in part because of the abuses that took place in
Corinth and Paul's stern rebuke (which we will examine shortly).

Like the Jewish synagogue service, the Christian worship liturgy
contained a heavy dose of Scripture reading and prayer. The early
church "devoted themselves to the apostles' teaching and to the fellowship, to the breaking of bread and to prayer" (lit. "the prayers";
Acts 2:42), and these probably comprised the major worship elements of the early Christian gatherings.[2] The "prayers" were ceremonial Jewish prayers, for the earliest believers in that day were Jew-

---

1. P. T. O'Brien, "Church," in *Dictionary of Paul and His Letters*, eds. Hawthorne et
   al., 125, thinks that references to "the whole church" (Rom. 16:23; 1 Cor. 14:23)
   suggest multiple house churches in the vicinity of Corinth that occasionally came
   together for worship.
2. I. Howard Marshall, *Acts*, Tyndale New Testament Commentaries (Grand Rapids: Eerdmans, 1989), 83; see also I. H. Marshall, *Last Supper and Lord's Supper* (Grand Rapids:
   Eerdmans, 1980), 127; and J. Jeremias, *The Eucharistic Words of Jesus*, trans. N. Perrin

ish. The apostles' teaching reflected their exposition of Scripture as it applied to the coming of Jesus Messiah. These two elements—Scripture reading and prayer—became so central for Paul that he insisted that the next generation of preachers faithfully continue their practice. In Christian worship men are to "lift up holy hands in prayer" (1 Tim. 2:8) and Timothy was to "devote" himself to the public reading of Scripture (1 Tim. 4:13). This reading of Scripture may have been accompanied by what Paul calls "prophecy," i.e., "prophetic preaching."[3] Whatever the nature and abuses of prophecy turn out to be in the New Testament, its intended purpose was for the edification of the church (1 Cor. 14:1-5).

Christians regularly observed the Lord's Supper as the focal point of the service, as Jesus commanded them (Lk. 22:19; 1 Cor. 11:23-25), and sang hymns (1 Cor. 14:26; Col. 3:16; Eph. 5:18-20; Acts 16:25). Paul may have even included a few of these hymns in his letters (e.g., Phil. 2:6-11; Col. 1:15-20; Eph. 5:14; 1 Tim. 3:16).[4] Paul instructed the Corinthians and several churches in Galatia (1 Cor. 16:1-2) that during the service they should also take up an offering as a gift to help alleviate the famine hitting the Jerusalem churches. The first-century Christian worship service in Paul's experience and in his churches reflects the Jewish elements of devotion to Scripture (perhaps with accompanying exposition), and prayer, but also included hymn-singing (with reference to Christ), financial giving, baptism for new converts (as a ritual of cleansing and incor-

(Philadelpha: Fortress, 1966), 118-119. Jeremias suggests the term "devoting themselves" (*proskarterountes*) denotes regular visits to the synagogue in the Coptic Texts.

3. Anthony Thiselton, *The Living Paul: An Introduction to the Apostle's Life and Thought* (Downers Grove, IL: InterVarsity Press, 2009), 111-112. New Testament prophecy wasn't generally predictive (though cf. Acts 11:27-28, 21:10-11), but rather God-inspired exhortation at a level above that of normal preaching. It was certainly more than exposition of the text. See Max Turner, *The Holy Spirit and Spiritual Gifts* (Peabody, MA: Hendrickson, 1996), 187; G. Friedrich, "*prophētēs, ktl,*" in *Theological Dictionary of the New Testament*, eds. Kittel and Friedrich, 6:848-853.

4. Scholars generally agree that these are liturgical hymns sung in the early Pauline churches, but cannot agree on whether Paul wrote them himself or incorporated them from well-known Christian traditions.

poration into the body of Christ and the fulfillment of the hopes of Israel[5]), and centrally the observance of the Lord's Supper, which gave worship new significance for Paul in the Christian community.[6]

At Worship in the Synagogue

Paul's consistent practice of worship began in his youth, most likely through the raising of his parents. Being raised in the scrupulous tradition of the Pharisees, Paul regularly attended synagogue services and heard the Law read aloud on a regular basis. Scripture reading (and sometimes its exposition) was the central focus of the synagogue service, accompanied by prayer and perhaps some associated singing.[7] Though we have no hard evidence in either Acts or the Epistles regarding Paul's attendance at synagogue in his youth, it's hard to imagine Paul *not* regularly attending synagogue services.

Paul didn't forsake worship in the synagogue once he became a believer, though. Paul frequented the synagogue even after his conversion (Acts 13:5, 14–15, 42–44; 14:1; 16:13; 17:2, 10, 17; 18:4, 19; 19:8). Aside from the dozen or so explicit references to Paul's worshiping in the synagogue, Luke notes that it was Paul's "custom" to do so (Acts 17:2; cf. 14:1). He even visited the temple (Acts 21:26–27) whenever he could to worship with his fellow Jews and to preach Christ from the Scriptures. His reasons for continuing to worship in the synagogue have nothing to do with nostalgia. Rather, Paul

---

5. McKnight, *A Community Called Atonement*, 149–152; Jon A. Weatherly, "The Role of Baptism in Conversion: Israel's Promises Fulfilled for the Believer in Jesus," in *Evangelicalism and the Stone-Campbell Movement*, vol. 1, ed. William R. Baker (Downers Grove, IL: InterVarsity Press, 2002), 159–175.

6. For a brief discussion of the components of the Christian worship service, particularly as they find their new expression in worship of Jesus, see Hurtado, *Lord Jesus Christ*, 137–151.

7. The first-century synagogue service was characterized primarily by the reading of Scripture and ceremonial prayers. Evidence for singing in the Jewish synagogue service is scant. See the discussion and related material in my *The Spirituality of Jesus*, 74–75.

continued to frequent the synagogue for more theological reasons, specifically because of what he believed about the people of God.

Paul, Worship, and the People of God

You don't have to peruse the bookshelves very long at your modern Christian bookstore, or listen very long on your local Christian radio station, or attend many services in the average modern American church to come across this basic truth: Ours is a *personal* spirituality. Our theology is personal: God created the world for *my* enjoyment. I pray to him for *my own* needs. Our view of Jesus's mission is personal: Jesus died for *my* sin and put *me* back in a proper relationship with the Father. We read the Scriptures personally: "What does this mean for *me?*" Even our worship is personal: I go to the house of God to sing praises in music *I* like and to hear God speak to *me* a personal word to live *my* life for him the rest of the week. Eugene Peterson describes this kind of spirituality as "little more than self-help psychology with a little holy water sprinkled over it."[8] It was bound to happen. Our nation is highly individualistic, where going it alone is a display of strength and stamina. And it was bound to spill over into our spirituality, our theology, and even into our worship.

In contrast to our modern, individualistic notions, Paul's vision of salvation has very *corporate* (i.e., "group") overtones. Given the number of times that Paul invokes the story of Abraham in his letters (Rom. 4:1-3, 9-25, 11:1; Gal. 3:6-14, 16, 4:21-31), it seems best to start there. God had promised Abraham a son, even though his wife was barren, and through that son Abraham would be the father of "many nations" (Gen. 17:4; cf. 17:5-6). Of course, through Isaac's line comes Jacob and his twelve sons, and the race of people we know as the Jews. Paul's Jewish training taught him that "salvation is from the Jews" (Jn. 4:22), and that Gentiles were excluded from the people of God. But the promise given to Abraham was "*All nations* will be blessed through you" (Gal. 3:8; cf. Gen.

---

8. Eugene H. Peterson, *The Wisdom of Each Other* (Grand Rapids: Zondervan, 1998), 73.

12:3, 18:18, 22:18, emphasis mine), not just the Jews, but *all nations* who believe on Jesus. God has been building a people for himself since the time of Abraham, and though the promise originally comes *through* the Jewish bloodlines (Rom. 2:9-10; Mt. 10:5-6), it was never intended to be *exclusively* Jewish, for the Scriptures continually point to the time when God's salvation would be extended to the Gentiles,[9] and in the words of Isaiah, that "all peoples" and "all nations" might be "*his* people" (Isa. 25:6-8, emphasis mine).

Paul's descriptions of salvation are more corporate than individualistic, hinting toward the fact that in Christ Jews and Gentiles are saved into one people, one family. Consider Ephesians 2:8-9, which most evangelicals can quote by heart: "For it is by grace you have been saved, through faith—and this is not from yourselves, it is the gift of God—not by works, so that no one can boast." We tend to read it as a manifesto of personal salvation and peace with God. But the "you" in those verses is plural ("you all"), and Paul says in the next few verses that Gentiles ("uncircumcised") who were excluded from membership in the people of God are now part of the People (2:11-13). Evoking the imagery of the wall in the temple that separated the court of Israel from the court of the Gentiles, Paul declares that God has "destroyed the barrier, the dividing wall of hostility" (Eph. 2:14).[10] There are now no divisions between Jew and Gentile, but both are part of the people of God, and both have access to "the temple" and the sacrifice of Christ through faith.

---

9. For a brief overview, see Kaiser, *Mission in the Old Testament.*
10. This is the view of F. F. Bruce, *The Epistles to the Colossians, to Philemon, and to the Ephesians,* New International Commentary on the New Testament (Grand Rapids: Eerdmans, 1984), 296-298. While he mentions several who adopt this view, H. W. Hoehner, *Ephesians: An Exegetical Commentary* (Grand Rapids: Baker, 2002), 369-374, is more cautious, identifying the "dividing wall" as much more than the physical partition in the temple, but a metaphor for the Law. P. T. O'Brien, *The Letter to the Ephesians,* Pillar New Testament Commentary, ed. D. A. Carson (Grand Rapids: Eerdmans, 1999), 195-196, concurs. Paul certainly mentions the Law as causing division between Jews and Gentiles (Eph. 2:15), but it would not be out of character for Paul to see the dividing wall in the temple as one external manifestation among many which derive from the Law.

Paul concludes by declaring that Gentiles are "no longer foreigners and aliens, but *fellow citizens* with God's people and *members of God's household*" (2:19, emphasis mine).

This emphasis upon the people of God is peppered throughout Paul's letters. Paul writes to the Colossians that "God's chosen people" are now comprised of Greek and Jew, circumcised and uncircumcised, barbarian, Scythian, slave and free (Col. 3:11-12). He echoes the same to the Galatians, that salvation in Christ Jesus does not separate Jew from Greek, slave from free, or male from female. All who belong to Christ are the heirs of the promise originally given to Abraham (Gal. 3:28-29). A clue to Paul's thought shows up subtly in 1 Corinthians 12:2, where Paul says, literally, "when you were pagans." He considers them pagans no longer.[11] Paul's view is most fully developed in Romans 9-11, and much of the theological wrangling that ensues over these chapters would benefit from an understanding that Paul is trying to speak of Jews and Gentiles as *one people of God*, and not (to Paul's dismay) that Israel has some special privileges or that the Gentiles have replaced Israel as the chosen people of God. In Paul's view, those who believe on Christ, whether they be Jew or Gentile, are all "God's chosen people" (Col. 3:12; cf. Rom. 9:24-26).

That is not to discount the personal aspect of salvation, much of which is in view in the early chapters of Romans. The wages of sin is death (Rom. 6:23) and no single individual is righteous before God (Rom. 3:10, 20) apart from the righteousness revealed in Christ Jesus (Rom. 3:21-24). God came to save individual sinners, and apparently Paul considered himself at the top of the "Ten Most Sinful" list (1 Tim. 1:15). This is how we've come to read the New Testament in the Protestant church, and the personal aspects cannot be denied. But our personal salvation is now in need of a theology of *community*, an understanding that Paul spoke in terms of *one people of God* comprised of both Jew and Gentile.

---

11. For a brief discussion on this see Hays, *Echoes of Scripture in the Letters of Paul*, 96.

If the people of God are *one*, and not two (i.e., Jew and Gentile),[12] then Paul's major concern for the church is that of its corporate unity, especially during its weekly gathering. The church is to be united as one body and not segregated by race, economic status, gender, or even spiritual giftedness. This unity comes through the Spirit (Eph. 4:3), who is present in the gathering of the local church (1 Cor. 5:4). This "Spiritual" unity was so strong in Paul's mind that he found himself united with believers in other churches during the appointed hour for worship even when he couldn't be with them physically (1 Cor. 5:3). This unity among believers, and our loving concern for one another, was the prayer of Jesus (Jn. 17:21–22), and Paul works hard to build it and encourage it among his churches. So central to the well-being of Christ's church was this unity that Paul regularly disciplined elements in his churches that threatened the unity of God's people.

Threats to Unity

Once you see this emphasis that Paul had upon building one-covenant people it becomes a bit easier to see why Paul was adamant about reigning in worship practices and attitudes that caused divisions among the people during worship. The problems Paul spent the most time addressing threatened to disrupt the unity he was trying to build and further divide the people of God from one another.

Consider the problems in Corinth surrounding the observance of the Lord's Supper. Divisions within the Corinthian church were rife (1 Cor. 1:1–17; 3), possibly because of some desire among the people to be more "spiritual" than either

---

12. This is the argument of Galatians 3:19–20, where Paul picks up on the tradition of the Law having been given through mediators. A mediator does not represent just one party, but two. If God is one party, then there cannot be two *other* parties (i.e., Jew and Gentile), but only one remaining party—the people of God. See Wright, *The Climax of the Covenant*, 157–174; F. F. Bruce, *Epistle to the Galatians*, New International Greek Testament Commentary (Grand Rapids: Eerdmans, 1982), 178–179.

other members of the Corinthian church or other churches in the area.[13] Their divisions and hyper-spirituality were becoming manifest in the way they observed the Lord's Supper. Following Roman meal customs, the host of the meal (probably a wealthy person with a larger home) invited the honored guests to dine in the parlor with better, more expensive food, while less honored guests were given seats in the outlying rooms with food of a lesser quality. "The whole thing became class-ridden and divisive."[14] This was neither unified nor loving, and Paul chides them, "I have no praise for you, for your meetings do more harm than good" (1 Cor. 11:17). He tried to correct these abuses by calling his readers to recognize the corporate "body of the Lord" (i.e., the community, not Jesus's flesh; 1 Cor. 11:29) and to remember that when the Israelites came out of the desert there was no special food or drink to separate the commoner from the "spiritual" person. "They all ate the same spiritual food and drank the same spiritual drink" (1 Cor. 10:3-4).[15]

Consider also the comments that Paul makes about women praying or prophesying with their heads uncovered in the corporate worship service (1 Cor. 11:3-16). A woman's hair was her pride and a primary instrument in luring men for romance. Roman women often pinned up their hair in elaborate styles as a display of either sexuality or status. Universal etiquette in the first century required women to cover their hair during worship

---

13. So Anthony C. Thiselton, *First Corinthians: A Shorter and Exegetical Commentary* (Grand Rapids: Eerdmans, 2006), 170–171.

14. See Thiselton, *The Living Paul*, 124; Thiselton, *First Corinthians*, 20, 181–182.

15. Mark Krause, "The Lord's Supper in the New Testament," in *Evangelicalism and the Stone-Campbell Movement*, vol. 2, ed. William R. Baker (Abilene, TX: ACU Press, 2006), 169: "The repeated *to auto* (*the same*) should not be seen as saying that the wilderness Israelites celebrated the Lord's Supper like the Corinthians. The 'sameness' refers to the historical fact that all the Israelites ate the same fare: manna and water. No 'bread of breads' and 'drink of drinks' was reserved for leadership or priesthood. Only one item appeared on the daily menu for all of them, and one choice for beverage. What this reveals is the unity that Paul finds in the act of eating and drinking the Lord's Supper as the gathered people of God."

assemblies, and it was true for pagan worship as well.[16] Some women in Corinth were taking too much license, violating the entire world's standards of propriety and holiness, and showing up to worship without head coverings. So Paul craftily argues with them that, just as it would be shameful for men to wear head coverings in worship, so also it was shameful for women to pray and prophesy without them (1 Cor. 11:4–5). He sarcastically remarks (as he does in Galatians 5:12) that if they wanted to be so disrespectful as to prophesy with their heads "uncovered," they ought to finish the job and shave their heads. Perhaps the specifics are cultural, but Paul's universal principle is timeless: Seduction, class distinctions, and hubris are not appropriate for corporate worship. They destroy unity (separating men from their rightful wives, and men from one another in jealousy) and eschew the honor and reverence with which God is to be approached. Paul warned his readers (ancient and modern) that those who disagree with him on this matter are being contentious with God (1 Cor. 11:16). Both men and women in our own day should take note of Paul's warnings here that corporate worship (of which prayer is an integral part) be separated from our attempts to dress better than others, to seduce would-be suitors, or to demonstrate independence from our spouses (the helpmates God has given to us). Worship is for God and is to be done for "the good of others" (1 Cor. 10:24), with a view toward the unity of the body, and not for the advancement of self.

The Corinthians' use of spiritual gifts was to be done with acknowledgment that those gifts were not to be used for self-aggrandizement, but for the building up of the body of Christ (1 Cor. 12:7–11), recognizing that each of us has different gifts that all originate from the same source (1 Cor. 12:4–6). Not all

---

16. For more on head coverings, see Craig Keener, "Man and Woman," in *Dictionary of Paul and His Letters*, eds. Hawthorne et al., 585–586; see also Keener, *1–2 Corinthians*, The New Cambridge Bible Commentary (Cambridge: Cambridge University Press, 2005), 90–94.

are apostles or teachers or prophets (1 Cor. 12:29–30), but "we were all baptized by one Spirit into one body . . . and we were all given the one Spirit to drink" (1 Cor. 12:13). Paul's corrections regarding the disharmony of those in Corinth put his comments in the famous "love chapter" (1 Cor. 13) into different perspective. Paul is not touting the awesomeness of love as a romantic emotion, but rather challenging the Corinthians to *demonstrate* love for one another in how they behave—to be patient and kind with one another, to stop boasting about their advantages and seeking their own interests, and to treat one another with trust (1 Cor. 13:4–7).

This same undercurrent—this desire to see the people of God unified and not divided or ostracized—also appears in Paul's counsel to Timothy, in a chapter that seems to have propriety in the corporate worship service as its theme.[17] He instructs that men "lift up holy hands in prayer" (1 Tim. 2:8), not in anger or brawling (as men tend to do when they "lift hands"). He instructs that women dress appropriately, not in the sexually promiscuous manner of the "priestitutes" in the temple of Artemis there in Ephesus (who dressed with braids, gold, pearls, and expensive clothing, 1 Tim. 2:9), for, like the situation in Corinth, this would cause divisions between men and their wives, create jealousies among men and women, and destroy the unity and holiness that God desires in the church. Regardless of the many possible interpretations still given about Paul's counsel that the women remain silent in that church (1 Tim. 2:11–15), what is plainly evident is that the situation had become unruly and divisive, and Paul's comments are designed to restore unity to the body.

Paul, Unity, and the Modern Church
So what do we take away from Paul and his experience with

---

17. First Timothy 2 contains several indicators that Paul is giving instruction about behavior in the corporate worship service in Ephesus. For a detailed discussion, see George W. Knight III, *The Pastoral Epistles*, New International Greek Testament Commentary (Grand Rapids: Eerdmans, 1992), 113–149.

church and synagogue in worship? We've considered what the first-century service was like and what mattered to Paul. It's time now to consider some applications that will ground our worship experiences and practices in the same kind of honor and integrity that Paul demonstrated and expected from the church of God.

First, Paul attended worship believing that Jesus would be there. It's easy to fall into the trap of treating worship as a ceremonial duty—as something that has to be done in order to appease God's jealous nature. Sometimes I go to church because it's what's expected of me; and if I'm honest, there are times when going is tedious and lifeless, even boring. I think there are times when God honors religious duty and appreciates the fact that I go when I don't always want to. Paul, though, had a profound expectation that when he joined the people of God in worship, the Spirit of Jesus was present (1 Cor. 5:4). There was no praying that the Spirit *would* come, or inviting the Spirit to be a part of the ceremony. He expected that Jesus would make good on his word, that "where two or three come together in my name, there I am with them" (Mt. 18:20). Part of the solution to the occasional doldrums of worship is to recognize that, when I stand in the midst of God's people in the worship service, the Spirit of Jesus is there also, actively moving, convicting (Jn. 16:7–11), gifting the body (1 Cor. 12:4–11), even encouraging and promoting fellowship among believers (Phil. 2:1–2).

Second, worship is for glorifying God and edifying the body of believers. Our church culture is saturated with the drive for numerical growth. The local church seems these days to be more interested in programs and events that get more and more people in the door and less concerned with whether or not those programs honor God and help pilgrims walk the way of Jesus. We've grown accustomed to planning services that honor various individuals within our churches and communities, occasionally giving more honor to them than to the One for whom this service was dedicated. The "booths of the sons of Annas" (the franchise of money-changers Jesus disrupted in the temple) are still prominent in our own temples, placing success alongside obedience. Always lurking is the temptation for the one preaching to placate, to ignore the whole counsel of God in order to win over and appease the masses. Like Paul, we want to "become all things to all men" (1 Cor. 9:22). But truth be told, we sometimes do these things only to foster the appearance of success. We would do well to remember that Paul's churches were mostly house churches, that success in Paul's eyes was about being *obedient* to Christ, and that Jesus was also tempted to compromise the true worship of God in the name of kingdom advancement (Mt. 4:8-10). In Paul's view, worship was about making Jesus look good (which the Bible calls "glorifying"; cf. 1 Cor. 14:22-25) and building one another up in the faith (Eph. 4:11-13).

Which brings us to the final point: *The unity of the church is of critical importance.* Jesus articulated the greatest commandments, the summation of all that God wants from us, in the love of God and the loving care for one another (Mt. 22:37-40; Mk. 12:29-31). If these are the two greatest concerns for the church, then it stands to reason that churches will be tempted, in both large and small ways, to abandon their mission in these two areas. We will be tempted to allow things that are not directly honoring to God and practices and policies that separate us from one another and cause division to creep into our worship. If love of God and neighbor are the two greatest commandments, then the lure to abandon them will be the two greatest temptations.

The things that divide the people of God from one another are many. They are intertwined with race; economic status; political affiliation; personal preferences about music style, preaching style, furniture style, and liturgy; nonessential points of theology; and a whole host of things that Paul would likely challenge in our churches if they tended to destroy corporate unity.

Let me give you one example of how subtle changes in worship can lead to division among the people of God, and how we must do everything in our power to prevent this division: I served for a while in a church located in a major metropolitan area. We had members from all kinds of places: the United States, Puerto Rico, Mexico, Jamaica, Haiti, Guyana, Panama, Portugal, Canada, Brazil, and Argentina. Race had never been an issue in our congregation, and when we gathered for worship, we were a living portrait of John's throne-room scene in Revelation 5, as people from every tribe and language gathered around the throne together in unified worship. Knowing that our community was heavily populated with speakers of Spanish, we embarked upon an evangelistic outreach to Spanish speakers to introduce them to Christ and incorporate them into the people of God. We thought it would be a good idea to provide them a completely separate worship service, one in which they could worship in their native language. So we offered a Spanish-speaking service for those who wanted to attend, and asked those who could and were willing to attend that service rather than the others we offered. That service was completely different from the other two we offered, and in reality removed one people group from the main services.

It was a mistake and a failure on our part. What seemed like a noble attempt at evangelism actually separated a certain segment of our congregation from the life of the church. In a very short year, our hopes of "an open door" of missionary activity (Rev. 3:8) degenerated into racial infighting, jealousy, and bitter divisiveness between those who were in leadership and those who had been (in their minds) ostracized from the corporate gathering of the church. We couldn't see it for the longest time, and by the time we did, it had almost destroyed the church. Looking back, we now see how our approach separated one segment of the community from the other. We did away with the separate service and returned to a unified, corporate worship *together*.

This is not to say that every church that provides a separate service is wrong to do so. The church I currently attend is doing this quite successfully and without threat to the unity of the body. This is simply a personal illustration about a situation that one church faced and what it meant for us. It is illustrative, however, of the *kinds* of things that take place in churches. Jesus's prayer was that we all be one, as he is one with the Father (Jn. 17:21–23). Perhaps instead of focusing our attention on how we can be successful, we might do well to spend our time on defining success in terms of faithfulness to God and corporate unity. Jesus said with his own lips that our effectiveness in evangelism would be commensurate with our ability to love and care for one another (Jn. 13:35).

■

CHAPTER 7

"Holy and Blameless in His Sight": Holiness

■ ASK TEN SERIOUS, COMMITTED CHRISTIANS who are well-read in Scripture about holiness, and you're likely to get the same answer: "The Bible commands it." Students of the Word are in universal agreement that God is holy, and he expects his people to be holy. The command is found over and again in Scripture, "I am the LORD your God; consecrate yourselves and be holy, because I am holy" (Lev. 11:44, 19:2, 20:26; 1 Pet. 1:16).

But ask those same ten believers to define what that holiness entails, and you're likely to get ten different opinions. For centuries the definitions of holiness have wildly differed among the people of God. Some define holiness with an implied code of abstinence—withdrawing from the world and avoiding its ills—from alcohol, tobacco, gambling, R-rated movies, Halloween, and sometimes even caffeine, electricity, Christmas, rock/contemporary music, and television. These things (and many others) corrupt, they say, and avoiding them sets believers apart from the world and removes the roots of temptation. "*Avoid* these things, and you'll be holy" is the basic message.

Others have defined holiness in a more systematic fashion, creating elaborate policies for their disciples to follow in order to foster the underlying conditions that create a more positive view of holiness. "*Do* these things, and you'll be holy." The desert monks in the early church period got fed up with the laxity of their churches and fled to the desert to be holy. They quickly developed complicated rules to govern their societies, to prevent them from becoming what they went to the desert to avoid, and to present themselves to God as pure.[1] These systems promote a more positive view of holiness, but tend to demand the same rigid obedience as their abstinence counterparts. Their descendants are alive and well in our day, still creating rigid systems of spirituality under the guise of holiness.

Paul hardly laid down any systematic rules of holiness (like the ones described above) for his readers. He understood holiness, to be sure. He knew that he was to be "set apart" (the definition of "holy") *from* his sinful life and set apart *unto* the Lord. He gives his readers plenty of illustrations, metaphors, and instruction[2] on how to live the holy life. But because of the occasional nature of Paul's letters, we don't find any systematic instruction about the rules of holiness. What we do find, however, is Paul's unwavering opinion that God expects his people to be holy in response to the salvation that he has so graciously given.

Paul and Holiness

As a Pharisee (Acts 23:6, 26:5; Phil. 3:5) and the son of a Pharisee (Acts 23:6), Paul was raised on a brand of holiness that was characterized by *external behavior*. The Pharisees (whose name meant "separatist") garnered their reputation by rigorously separating themselves from the Greek influences introduced into Judaism

---

1. See, for instance, the *Long Rules* of Basil the Great (c. 358), one of the first monastic rule-books, or the *Rule of St. Benedict* (480–547). P. Rousseau, "The Desert Fathers, Antony and Pachomius," in *The Study of Spirituality*, eds. Cheslyn Jones, Geoffrey Wainwright, and Edward Yarnold (Oxford: University Press, 1986), 120, reminds us that while some monks went to the desert to be alone, many went there to form a new society, a new community of devoted believers, and the sanctity of that community had to be guarded with rules.
2. Paul does give his readers several commands and instructions: 1 Cor. 7:17, 11:17, 34, 16:1; 1 Thess. 4:2; 2 Thess. 3:6, 10, 12. What I speak of here is any *systematic* and *categorized* schema of holiness.

by Herod the Great[3] and imposing upon all Jews the holiness expected of the priests who entered the temple.[4] In addition to avoiding the major sins (like sexual immorality, idolatry, etc.) they fasted
on Mondays and Thursdays, required the ceremonial washing of
hands before meals, created an elaborate system of oaths to govern
right speech, tithed everything (down to the spices), and refused to
share meals with Gentiles. They prayed in ways that were designed
to impress, and gave alms with public show. The "prayer of the
heart" was foreign to them. Their brand of holiness was external
and ceremonial. By contrast, Jesus's vision for holiness was less
about public show and the minutiae of "mint, dill, and cumin,"
but focused on the *internal* items of "justice, mercy and righteousness" (Mt. 23:23), fleshed out in action. He praised the Pharisees
for looking good on the outside, but criticized them for being holy
in appearance only. Inside, they were full of wickedness, hypocrisy,
and death (Mt. 23:27–28). Once Paul became a disciple of Jesus, he
bought into Jesus's vision of holiness. Internal renewal of the heart
by the Holy Spirit created the conditions that led to his holiness,
and not vice versa. Paul's holiness began on the inside.

     That doesn't mean that Paul abandoned the ceremonial, ex-
ternal aspects of holiness. Holiness that begins in the heart must
eventually work itself outward into the hands, and Paul seems just
as concerned for the purity of the sacred things in his Christian
days as he was before. Jews in Jerusalem specifically accused Paul
of defiling the holy place (the temple). They had leveled the same
charge against Stephen (Acts 6:13–14), and now accused Paul of
defiling the temple by teaching against it and bringing Gentiles into
the court of Israel (Acts 21:28; 24:6). Of course, it wasn't true (Acts
21:29). Even though Paul seems to have bought into Jesus's re-de-
fined vision of what it means to be the temple of God (Jn. 2:19–21;

---

3. This is how Eugene H. Peterson characterizes their movement in *The Jesus Way*
   (Grand Rapids: Eerdmans, 2007), 201–210.
4. This is how Meeks describes the philosophy and approach of the Pharisees in *The
   First Urban Christians*, 97.

1 Cor. 6:19), he was still a Jew, and would not desecrate that which was sacred or devoted to God. When he wanted to take Timothy along on his missionary journeys he circumcised Timothy (who was part Jew) as the Law commanded (Acts 16:3) and took vows in the prescribed Jewish custom (Acts 18:18). Paul joined in purification rites with other Jewish Christians in order to publicly demonstrate that he had not defiled the temple (Acts 21:23–24). Even though Paul was accused of sullying that which was holy, the driving rhetoric of Luke's narrative is that Paul was innocent of all charges. Paul's accusers cannot make their fictitious case against him (Acts 24:12), and the constant refrain that drives the story is "this man has done nothing deserving death" (Acts 25:25, 26:31; cf. 28:18).

Paul was innocent of the accusations leveled against him, and as a result he could speak of his conscience being clear before God. In Paul's view, the conscience was given to every person by the creator God to establish basic right and wrong (Rom. 2:14–15; 1 Tim. 1:5, 3:9; 2 Tim. 1:3) and constantly shows up in the pastoral Epistles as the thing which evil men set aside first in order to perpetrate their madness (1 Tim. 1:19–20, 4:2; Titus 1:15). Paul's holiness, exuded in everyday living, was such that he could speak of his conscience being clear in everything he did (Rom. 9:1; 1 Cor. 4:4; 2 Cor. 1:12). Even when the high priest ordered that Paul be struck before the Sanhedrin, Paul confidently asserted that his duty had been fulfilled in good conscience and that he was more innocent before God than the high priest (Acts 23:1–3).

Before he met Jesus Paul understood holiness in Pharisaic terms. But in his Christian life Paul demonstrated a holiness that was completely different. He lived a life that honored Christ, but not because he sought to garner God's favor. Paul believed that he already had God's favor because he was in Christ. God had *made* him holy. The proper response was to honor this with an appropriate lifestyle.

Made Holy to Be Holy

Paul offered himself to Christ Jesus in a holy and sacred way.

But it wasn't simply ceremonial and external. Paul saw holiness beginning *internally*, just as Jesus did. It began with a change of heart, a shift in identity and personhood that was wrought through the Spirit of God at his conversion. God has "poured out his love into our hearts by the Holy Spirit" (Rom. 5:5; cf. 2 Cor. 1:22), who now dwells within us (Eph. 3:17; 1 Cor. 6:19; 2 Cor. 6:16). The kind of holiness that Paul cut his teeth on could not lead to true righteousness, for the written code of holiness kills; only the Spirit of God gives life (2 Cor. 3:6), and any lasting holiness comes from the Spirit's inner workings.

One of the most important things to note when it comes to this radical shift in Paul's view is his belief that God *took the initiative*. We've been *made* holy, worked over from the inside out in ways that we could never accomplish on our own. Our response to God's initiative is a life of holiness in gratitude.

Paul used several images to communicate this change to his readers. Having once been *enslaved* to sin, passion, and desire (Rom. 6:15–23; 8:1–2; Titus 3:3), God set us *free*, and our response is to resist becoming enslaved that way again (Rom. 6:18, 22) and to devote ourselves to doing good (Titus 3:8). Having *died* in our sins (Eph. 2:1; Col. 2:13), God *raised* us to live a new life (Rom. 6:1–4; Eph. 2:4-6; Col. 2:13; 3:1). We were once in *darkness* (Eph. 5:8; Col. 1:13), but now we are *light* (Eph. 5:8; 1 Thess. 5:4–5) and must abandon things that people do in the dark (i.e., at night; spiritually sleep and get drunk) and be alert and sober, as people normally are in the light of day (1 Thess. 5:6–8; cf. Rom. 13:11–14). Formerly *enemies* of God and *excluded* from his promises (Eph. 2:11–12), now he has made *peace* with us through Christ and *included* us in those promises (Eph. 2:13–19). The grateful response is to present ourselves "holy in his sight, without blemish and free from accusation" (Col. 1:22), a holy temple rising to the Lord (Eph. 2:21). Where once our righteousness was as "filthy rags" (Isaiah 64:6), now we have been clothed with Christ's righteousness, having taken off the old self and put on the new (Col. 3:9–10). The newly clothed self consists of "putting on" humility, gentleness, and patience (Col. 3:12) and "taking off" a whole litany of sinful behavior (Eph. 4:17–5:20; Col. 3:7–8).

God has done the hard work of salvation and has wrought it in our hearts by his Spirit (the internal). Our response is to live in a manner worthy of that salvation (the external), to work hard at conforming our sinful "flesh" (a term for Paul that is inclusive of the entire sinful self) to the Spirit actively working inside us to make us holy. This response to salvation is as old as Isaiah, and Paul knew it. After the long-awaited salvation of God finally comes to Israel, and is announced on the mountains as "good news," the command rings out, "Depart, depart, go out from there! Touch no unclean thing! Come out from it and be pure" (Isa. 52:7–11; cf. 2 Cor. 6:17). Those who are thankful for the salvation God brings willingly offer him a lifestyle of holy living as a grateful response.

The Holiness Code

So what does this holiness look like? Is it just about abstaining from stuff? And if so, what? When considering the spirituality of Jesus, we had no cause to consider what holiness looks like for the average believer because Jesus was sinless. I can't imitate him in sin-less living. (I blew that a *long* time ago!) But in Paul we find a sinner who took the code of Jesus upon his life and lived it to the full. In Paul we have a mentor in Jesus-style holiness. Surely it involves being set apart *from* something, doesn't it? Absolutely it does. But it's a lot less work than you might think. And much more difficult to live.

I know what you're looking for. At this point, you're expecting me to outline for you a comprehensive system of holiness as I see it in Paul, to catalogue all of Paul's ethical demands and condense them into a system easily palatable for our twenty-first-century world. Several top-notch books have been written on this very subject, and I wholeheartedly recommend them.[5] But this truth must be set be-

---

5. Jerry Bridges, *The Pursuit of Holiness* (Colorado Springs: NavPress, 1978); Victor

fore us as believers in Christ-righteousness: "Holiness is *not* rules and regulations. Elaborate lists of dos and don'ts miss the point of a life hidden with God in Christ."[6] Boiling Paul's ethics down to a system will only cause us to create another list of rules and regulations from his commands. Paul's ethical demands upon his readers are not complex, but essentially boil down to a few simple principles.

On one level Paul's view of holiness originates with the Ten Commandments (excepting, per Jesus's teaching, the command regarding the Sabbath). In several places he challenges his readers to avoid idolatry, in accordance with the second commandment (Exod. 20:4–6; Rom. 1:23, 25; 1 Cor. 5:10–11; 6:9; 10:7, 19; 12:2; Gal. 5:20). He exhorts them to "put off falsehood and speak truthfully" (Eph. 4:25; cf. Col. 3:9) as an expression of the ninth commandment prohibiting false testimony (Exod. 20:16). His concerns about sexual immorality are the first-century expression of both the seventh commandment about adultery (Exod. 20:14) and the tenth commandment about coveting a man's spouse (Exod. 20:17). Even greed, which Paul suggests is the essence of idolatry (Col. 3:5), can be linked to the tenth commandment about covetousness. The Ten Commandments were the foundation of the Law as it was originally given, and around them the exceptional situations and special circumstances of the Law are built.[7]

On the other hand, though, scholars have long noted that the Ten Commandments bear a simple structure of respect for God and right relations with one another.[8] Basically, the Ten Commandments can be put in terms Paul learned from Jesus:

Paul Furnish, *The Moral Teaching of Paul* (Nashville: Abingdon, 1979); Derek Tidball, *The Message of Holiness* (Downers Grove, IL: InterVarsity Press, 2010).

6. Richard J. Foster, *Streams of Living Water* (San Francisco: HarperCollins, 1998), 83.

7. Peterson, *The Jesus Way*, 73–75, likens the holiness code in the Law to a set of signposts, delineating the boundaries of life in the kingdom.

8. Brevard S. Childs, *The Book of Exodus: A Critical Theological Commentary* (Philadelphia: The Westminster Press, 1974), 395; U. Cassuto, *A Commentary on the Book of Exodus*, trans. Israel Abrahams (Jerusalem: Magnes Press, 1983), 238–240; Victor P. Hamilton, *Handbook on the Pentateuch* (Grand Rapids: Baker, 1982), 200–201.

love of God and love of neighbor (Mk. 12:29-31). Some of his instructions regarding food laws have to do with meat offered in conjunction with idolatry, and Paul worked that out very carefully so that his believers reflected both an honest respect for God and a concern for the conscience and weakness of their fellow believers (Rom. 14:13-23; 1 Cor. 8:4-13). As Paul recounted the sins of humanity in Romans 1, many of the items on the list were characterized by a lack of love for other human beings (e.g., "envy, murder, strife, deceit and malice"; Rom. 1:29-30). The love of one another is the summation of the entire Law (Gal. 5:14) and it must have surely grieved the Father to see some of Paul's churches fighting amongst themselves (1 Cor. 1:10-17, 3:1; Phil. 4:2), dragging one another to court (1 Cor. 6:1-8), and treating the bride of Christ with contempt. Jesus warned that in whatever way we treated his "brothers," good or bad, he would take it personally.[9]

I wish that there were more space in a book like this to expound on every aspect of Paul's teaching and demonstrate how every command he gives falls along these categories. All of Paul's complex ethical demands can be summed up in these two simple directives: love God with all of your being, and show demonstrable respect for others. It's simple in scope and structure, but incredibly complex in its expression. Loving others means imitating Jesus in self-sacrifice, and the crucifixion of ego and selfish desires is an integral part in deferring to the needs of others. Devotion to Christ means living

---

9. The familiar refrain from the parable of the sheep and the goats, "whatever you did for one of the least of these brothers of mine, you did for me" (Mt. 25:40, cf. 25:45), has less to do with benevolent acts of mercy for humans and more to do with how believers treat one another. The "least of these" represents a word that is continually used in Matthew for the disciples, and the phrase "my brothers" calls to mind Jesus's statement that those who do the will of God (i.e., disciples) are Jesus's family (Mt. 12:46-50; Mk. 3:31-35; Lk. 8:19-21). The parable is told to the Twelve in private and seems to suggest that, as they ready themselves for Jesus's absence (Mt. 25:1-13) and put the message to work (Mt. 25:14-30), there will be those who either welcome them and their message or reject them. Either way, Jesus will take it personally and reward these hearers according to their responses to the disciples' message.

the Jesus-kind of life, complete with self-denial of one's own rights for the well-being of others. And being devoted *to* Jesus leads to a lot more holiness in Paul's view than abstaining *from* external influences that were made to be enjoyed in their proper contexts when consecrated by prayer and good conscience (1 Tim. 4:1-5).

Struggling with Holiness

Living a holy, godly life isn't easy, though. The old adage applies here: if it were easy, everyone would be doing it. We struggle against ourselves, our old ways of thinking, our fleshly desires, and the forces of darkness. We are the end-time people, and while we wait for the final curtain to drop, we still struggle to rein in the flesh and bring it in line with the Spirit's desires. There is hope, though, for in Paul's view the Holy Spirit is given to us for just that—holiness. He is the *Holy* Spirit, both representing God's holiness and working for ours. Scholars disagree about exactly how Paul views the work of the Spirit as it relates to making us holy (i.e., sanctification), but they generally acknowledge that when Paul refers to him as the "*Holy* Spirit" (instead of just "the Spirit") he tends to have holy living in view, suggesting that the Spirit leads us in right living.[10] Jesus told his disciples that the Spirit would guide us into all truth (Jn. 16:13), help us testify about Jesus (Jn. 15:26-27), remind us of the things that Jesus has said (Jn. 14:26), convict us when we need it (16:8-11), and bring us peace (14:27). The Spirit leads, we keep in step with him (Gal. 5:18, 25), and he helps us in our weakness (Rom. 8:26).

Paul knew the struggle. He said, "For in my inner being I delight in God's law; but I see another law at work in the members of my body, waging war against the law of my mind and making me a prisoner of the law of sin at work within my members. What a wretched man I am!" (Rom. 7:22-24). These two natures—that of flesh and that of the Spirit—continually worked in Paul so that

---

10. S. E. Porter, "Holiness, Sanctification," in *Dictionary of Paul and His Letters*, eds. Hawthorne et al., 400.

he wasn't always able to do the godly things he really wanted, and conversely sometimes did things he didn't want to do (Rom. 7:15, 19–20). His conclusion was that nothing good lived in him (Rom. 7:18), and that only Jesus could rescue him (Rom. 7:24–25) and set him free to live his life in the power of the Holy Spirit (Rom. 8:1–14). And he was confident that when he was tempted to go by another route, the Spirit would not let him be tempted beyond what he could bear (1 Cor. 10:13). Paul is brutally honest in this section of Romans as he recounts his own struggle to be holy.

For centuries this has been the traditional understanding of Romans 7:7–25–Paul's confession of his own struggle with sin. But there are those who claim that Romans 7:7–25 is not Paul's confession of his own sin, but rather a description of a person's pre-Christian life. In this view Paul is play-acting, helping us understand what a life enslaved to the Law is like. He seems to be saying, "Try to root out sin from your life through sheer willpower, without the aid of the Spirit given through faith in Christ, and you're doomed to continue doing the things you don't want to do and not do the things you want to do."[11] Pull yourself up by your bootstraps and you'll just get broken bootstraps. Admittedly, this *is* the flow of Paul's argument. Up to that point in Romans he has established that humanity is by nature sinful (Rom. 1–3), that God has made a way for us to be righteous in Christ (Rom. 3–4), that Christ has dealt with our tendency to sin inherited from Adam (Rom. 5), and that if you try to go by any other route than the one that Christ offers (especially the way of the Mosaic Law), it's doomed to failure and self-destruction (Rom. 7). Therefore, the only solution is to let Christ rescue you from this body of death and live life in the Spirit of God (Rom. 8). This is the gospel that he preaches to the Gentiles.[12]

Even if they are right, however, I can't see Paul *not* struggling

---

11. Fee, *Paul, the Spirit, and the People of God*, 133–135; Gorman, *Apostle of the Crucified Lord*, 371–373; Wright, *The Climax of the Covenant*, 196–200, 226–230.

12. Wright, *The Climax of the Covenant*, 195, contends that Paul is explaining his gospel to the Romans in this letter because he's never been there, and hopes to use the church

with sin. I can't see Paul, fiery personality that he was, controlling his tongue 100 percent of the time. I can't see him pushing himself so hard to work and to preach the gospel that he doesn't occasionally fail to recognize the toll that it takes upon his coworkers. And given the sheer number of people around him all the time, it's hard to think that there weren't some cross words spoken between him and them that needed mending from time to time. Perhaps I'm projecting my own sins onto the life of Paul. I can freely admit that. But no one knew the Law-based lifestyle better than Paul, and his musings about the wayward tendencies of the sinful nature in Romans 7 come from his own experience. He tried to live the Law and failed. His failure is identifiable to everyone who reads him. He wrote to sinful people, and his letters often address real-life problems that crept up in their struggle to live out the faith they had been so graciously given.

Being Holy with Paul

    I grew up in your typical "beer-cursing-tobacco" abstinence culture in central Kentucky. Both sets of grandparents were godly people, and they passed their holiness in everyday matters on to my parents, who passed them on to me and my sister. I was raised in the quintessential small-town church, complete with the stained-glass windows and the pipe organ. But the things I was taught at church that comprised holiness did not always agree with what I saw. I was taught at church and home that any consumption of alcohol was sinful. Alcohol was not permitted in my family. But everyone knew that my grandfather had kidney problems, for which he kept a fifth of whiskey in the back-porch refrigerator, and no one ever called him a sinner. The preacher taught me that smoking was a sin, but my dad smoked a pipe from time to time and my tobacco-farming grandfather always considered

---

in Rome as a missionary base for his ministry to the western parts of the empire (cf. Rom. 15:24–29), as he did Antioch in the east (Acts 13:1–3, 14:26, 15:35, 18:22–23).

a good crop a gift from the Lord. Porn was definitely out, and my father was conscientious enough to fast-forward through racy scenes in movies. But there was little discernment about what kinds of movies I was permitted to watch or what kinds of music I listened to. (Of course, until I got married I didn't know what most of the metaphors in my music meant!)

Please don't misunderstand what I am saying. I am *not* endorsing alcohol, tobacco, cursing, and R-rated movies as good, holy, and honorable. (Neither, if I'm honest and true to the text, can I deny that alcohol,[13] sensuality,[14] and a few choice words[15] appear in Scripture.) I don't drink, smoke, or gamble. (I must confess, though, I've seen the R-rated *Passion of the Christ.* Forgive me.) I grew up around tobacco, but I don't smoke. I spend my money on other things. I grew up watching horror movies. But at some point, they began to bother me, and I can tell you exactly the day and hour that I swore them off because they agitated the Spirit within me. I listen to a wider diversity of music than many of my colleagues, but there are still some things that I continually push aside because they are not God-honoring. I didn't get this way by creating complicated rules for myself. I

---

13. Jesus drank wine (see Luke 22:17–18, where "I will not drink *again*" implies that he had already), made it for others (Jn. 2:1–10), was accused of being a drunk (Mt. 11:19; Lk. 7:34), and compared his ministry to the likes of potent wine (Mt. 9:17; Mk. 2:22; Lk. 5:37–39; cf. Lk. 10:34). Paul specifically told Timothy to drink some wine (1 Tim. 5:23).

14. As he warns the Corinthians about sexual immorality, Paul wryly asks, "Shall I then take the members of Christ and unite them with a prostitute?" (1 Cor. 6:15). Paul told the Thessalonian men to "control their own body" (1 Thess. 4:4), a euphemism for the male sexual organ. David's indiscretion with Bathsheba is part of the scriptural record (2 Sam 11:1–5). The seeming sensuousness with which the Galilean prostitute anointed Jesus (letting down her hair, caressing his feet, and kissing him) is exactly what prompts the Pharisee's objection, "If this man were a prophet, he would know who is touching him and what kind of woman she is" (Lk. 7:39).

15. When Paul describes his old life of Judaism for the Philippians, he concludes by calling it "rubbish" (Phil. 3:8), a word which has overtones of "garbage," "refuse," "manure," or worse. See Wright, *Justification*, 149, who calls it "shockingly strong negative language."

devoted myself more and more to Christ, and along the way the Spirit began making me more and more uncomfortable with areas of my life that were not pure. The key to holiness in the Pauline tradition is not to make a system of rules, but rather to devote ourselves to Christ, to saturate ourselves with his Word, and to walk daily in the Spirit of God. The solution is not to say that all movies and music are bad, and neither is it to withdraw from all media. I have devoted my life to Christ, and the things that once consumed my attention have now been replaced by Scripture study, prayer, and proclamation of the Word (and cycling, and shooting droids with my kids on *Star Wars: Battlefront*).

Christian holiness, as Paul presents it, has less to do with what you abstain from and more to do with what you are devoted to. Derek Tidball sums it up well when he says that holiness "is as much about what we are as what we do, and it touches every aspect of life."[16] Holiness is about devotion, not abstinence—devotion to Christ, living a life of gratitude for him. Sometimes this leads to abstinence, and rightly so. But it is not the kind of "abstaining from things" that leads to favor with God. It stems from God's favor, already given in Christ, and a life worthy of the calling we have received. Sure, there are rules. The Law was given to preserve our holiness, but only until our coming of age in the Spirit (Gal. 3:24–4:5).[17] Since we now "live by the Spirit, let us keep in step with the Spirit" and live a life that is honoring to him (Gal. 5:25).

---

16. Tidball, *The Message of Holiness*, 23.
17. This seems to the meaning behind Paul's comments in this section of Galatians. The law was a "tutor" (*paidagōgos*) or a schoolmaster leading us to Christ. In the first-century world, the pedagogue was normally a slave responsible for both the education (mostly getting their charges to school, but occasionally teaching the children themselves) and protection of the master's children. Paul characterizes the Law as a pedagogue, both educating us and protecting us, until the time when we came of age ("when the time had fully come," Gal. 4:4) and received our inheritance (Gal. 4:1–5). Now that we are old enough to receive it, we are full sons and heirs of the promise (Gal. 4:6–7).

CHAPTER 8

■

"We Were All Given the One Spirit": Spiritual Gifts

■ I DON'T WORK IN THE NURSERY. It's not that I think that those who staff the nursery program in the local church are somehow lesser-class citizens than those who preach and teach. In fact, they are often some of the most loving, kindhearted and compassionate people in our church. Their sacrifice of worship is no less honorable than that given by the worship team or the soloist. What I *do* mean is that *I* don't work in the nursery, and unless there's a severe shortage of workers, you probably won't ever see me there. There are several reasons why I don't, but the main reason has nothing to do with my personality or my love of small children. The reason I don't work in the nursery is that God has gifted me in other areas.

The main area in which I'm gifted by the Spirit, confirmed over and over again by his people, is the area of teaching adults. I love the classroom. I love the give and take, the conversations among the students, the impromptu questions that challenge me to think biblically in new ways about new subjects. And I love the extended interaction we have week to week, whether it be in a Sunday school class, Wednesday night Bible study, or college classroom. Preaching is okay, but it's not as fun for me as teaching. I enjoy teaching the Bible, I'm trained for it, and the Spirit has confirmed through his people over the years that he's gifted me for it.

So I don't work in the nursery because God has gifted me to

do other things. If the Children's Ministry Coordinator called and said, "I have no one else for Sunday, and I'm desperate. Can you do it?" (and she has), then I would certainly do what I could to help out (and I have). It wouldn't be *great*, and she'd be scraping the bottom of the barrel when she asked me, but I would do it.

Sometimes we all have to serve in areas where we *aren't* gifted because God calls us to the task. But when God puts enough people in the church to do the numerous jobs that need to be done, I teach while others play the music, fix the roof, and staff the children's classrooms. What's more, I wholly recognize that on any given Wednesday night I couldn't teach the adults unless someone else was teaching their children.

This aspect of spiritual giftedness—the working together to benefit the entire church body—is probably the most important ingredient of Paul's teaching on the matter. There's a lot of literature out there on spiritual gifts, covering all the opinions about exactly what the gifts are, how they can be categorized (if at all), what good they serve, and which one particular individuals might have. But with the literature also comes confusion.

This is why we should turn to Paul for answers. No book on Paul's partnership with the Spirit would be complete without discussing the concept of spiritual gifts. Paul is the only writer in the New Testament to explicitly speak about spiritual gifts in any detail. He writes about the subject in three separate letters, suggesting that it's something he wanted the entire church to understand, not just one congregation. So to understand the gifts properly, we need to go straight to the source. In this chapter we'll spend some time considering what spiritual gifts are, what purpose they serve, and how we can best use them for their intended purpose.

The Language and Purpose of Spiritual Gifts

Just what is a spiritual gift? The language that Paul uses for spiritual gifts (Gk. *charismata*) is nothing mystical, but simply the word "gift."[1] That he uses the term, though, to describe the things that are given by the Spirit, along with their designated purpose within the spiritual community, naturally brings something "spiritual" to mind. He intends the "gift" language to be understood spiritually, for he also calls them "manifestation(s) of the Spirit" (1 Cor. 12:7), "service" (1 Cor. 12:5), "working(s)" of the Spirit (1 Cor. 12:6) and literally Spirit "things" (1 Cor. 12:1).

Paul lists the spiritual gifts in three places in his letters: 1 Corinthians 12–14, Romans 12, and Ephesians 4:7–13. In these passages he outlines a list of gifts, describes their purpose, and offers advice on how they are to be used in orderly worship. Before we get to the list of the gifts he mentions, two fundamental Pauline ideas must be pointed out.

First, *every believer has been gifted by the Spirit*. Paul points this out in all three of the passages concerning the gifts. "Now to *each one* the manifestation of the Spirit is given" (1 Cor. 12:7, emphasis mine). In the letter to the Romans Paul begins his discussion of the gifts by comparing the congregation to a human body. He reminds them that "we who are many form one body, and *each member* belongs to all the others" (Rom. 12:5, emphasis mine). He then describes their mutual dependence upon one another by pointing out that they have all been gifted differently (Rom. 12:6–8) and therefore need one another for a healthy "body". He doesn't say that some of them have been given gifts for which the church should be grateful, but rather emphasizes that everyone has been gifted by the Spirit for the common good, and that each person's gift is necessary to build the church. The same is in view in Ephesians where "each one of us" has been given grace (4:7), and that grace comes with an endowment of gifts (4:8). Paul else-

---

1. See Johannes P. Louw and Eugene A. Nida, *Greek-English Lexicon of the New Testament Based on Semantic Domains* (New York: United Bible Societies, 1989), 57.103; W. Bauer, W. F. Arndt, and F. Wilbur Gingrich, *Greek-English Lexicon of the New Testament and Other Early Christian Literature*, 1st ed. (Chicago: University of Chicago Press, 1957), 877.

where characterizes believers as those who have the Spirit (Rom. 8:9–11; 2 Cor. 1:22; Gal. 4:6; Eph. 1:13–14). Those who have the Spirit also have the gifts that he bestows.

Second, *spiritual gifts are given to build up the entire church*. Paul told the Corinthian church that "to each one the manifestation of the Spirit is given for the common good" (1 Cor. 12:7). God gave gifts "to prepare God's people for works of service, so that the body of Christ may be built up" (Eph. 4:12). Each of the spiritual gifts, in the ancient church and in the modern, is given for the common good of the congregation. No place exists for individual gifts which edify or benefit the giver alone. "These manifestations of the spirit are marked out for Paul as given (not achieved by man), as expressions of divine energy (not human potential or talent), as acts of service which promote the common good (not for personal edification or aggrandizement)."[2]

In Paul's view, the gifts have been given for a particular purpose. But that purpose is neither to provide believers with a unique talent or ability that sets them off from the world, nor to distinguish believers from one another like spiritual fingerprints. Rather, the purpose of the gifts is to allow their recipients to build up the congregation, be witnesses to the world, and encourage one another.

It's almost time to turn to a discussion of the spiritual gifts Paul mentions in his letters. But before we do that, we must set one more prop on the stage.

The Nature of Paul's Lists

The spiritual gifts that Paul mentions in his letters always appear in the midst of a list. Paul sometimes gives lengthy lists to describe his subject matter, piling up the vocabulary to give his readers a broad understanding of the topic at hand. These lists are not meant to give an exhaustive accounting of the subject matter,

---

2. James D. G. Dunn, "Spirit, Holy Spirit," in *New International Dictionary of New Testament Theology*, ed. Colin Brown (Grand Rapids: Zondervan, 1975), 3:703.

but work in a very different kind of way. So we have to understand the way Paul uses lists in his letters before we can accurately assess the lists of spiritual gifts he gives us.

Here's the thing you need to know about lists in Paul's letters: *Paul's lists are meant to be categorical and descriptive, not exhaustive.* In other words, when Paul includes a list of something in his letters, it's not so that he can write down every single idea and vocabulary word on the subject. His letters don't function that way or for that purpose. The lists appearing in his letters are more descriptive of the *types* of things he's speaking of rather than exhaustive of every single item included in that category. In other words, Paul's lists convey the *sense* or the *kinds* of things that he's trying to describe.[3]

For example, consider the sins of humanity that Paul lists in Romans 1:21–32. He describes things like sexual depravity (of both the heterosexual and homosexual varieties), idolatry, greed, envy, murder, deceit, slander, and disobedience toward parents. It's true that most of the sins of humanity can be found there. But I can think of a few sins that aren't on the list: pornography, pedophilia, abuse, drunkenness, and gluttony, just to name a few. Does Paul not consider gluttony a sin? Of course he does (Phil. 3:19). That he doesn't mention it in this list is a product of his purpose, not his forgetfulness. His list is not *exhaustive* (meaning he's not out to list every single sin that human beings commit; that would be impossible), but rather *categorical and descriptive* (meaning that he's recording the *kinds* of things that sinful people do).

Or consider the list of the "fruit of the Spirit" in Galatians 5:22–23. When the Spirit begins to work in a person's heart, the natural result is the demonstrated fruit of "love, joy, peace, patience, kindness, goodness, faithfulness, gentleness and self-con-

---

3. For more on the nature of Paul's lists as they relate to the gifts of the Spirit, see Ralph P. Martin, *The Spirit and the Congregation: Studies in 1 Corinthians 12–15* (Grand Rapids: Eerdmans, 1984), 13; F. F. Bruce, *1 and 2 Corinthians*, New Century Bible (London: Oliphants, 1971), 119.

trol." Paul concludes his thought by saying, "Against such things [lit. "these kinds of things"] there is no law." "The fact that Paul ends the list with *ta homoia toutois,* 'and such like,' shows us that it is by no means considered by him as exhaustive, but merely typical."[4] Is compassion not a fruit of the Spirit? Does the Spirit not make me a more merciful person? Of course he does. But again, what Paul includes are only the *kinds of things* the Spirit produces in the heart of a person, not an exhaustive list of every last piece of fruit that falls from the Spirit's tree.

I will not delineate them here, but the same thing could be said about the qualifications for elders and deacons that show up in 1 Timothy 3 and Titus 1. To treat them like a checklist to approve before the congregational vote is probably not what Paul had in mind. The things he mentions there absolutely apply, and not many an elder has been disqualified from leadership because one of his problems didn't fall under the umbrella of something Paul mentions in those lists. But we must keep in mind that, as Paul intended them, the qualifications served to denote the *kind of person* that God was looking for in leadership.

Which brings us around to the gifts of the Spirit. As Paul "lists" them in his various letters, he does not intend us to view the lists as an exhaustive description of every last gift bestowed upon believers in the church. Rather, the lists serve to demonstrate the *kinds* of gifts that the Spirit bestows upon individuals and churches for the advancement of the gospel and the edification of the church. There is some overlap between the lists, but not much, and the fact that Paul writes three different lists to three different churches suggests that the Spirit never intended us to view any or all of the lists as a complete compilation of the only gifts ever given to the church. Gordon Fee sums this aspect of Paul's lists up more than adequately when he says that "none of them is intended to be complete, as

4. R. Alan Cole, *Galatians,* Tyndale New Testament Commentaries (Downers Grove, IL: InterVarsity Press, 2007), 212.

though Paul were setting forth everything that might legitimately be called a 'gift of the Spirit.' This is proved in part by the fact that no two lists are identical. It goes beyond the evidence—and Paul's own concerns—to speak of 'the nine spiritual gifts.'"[5]

For seven and a half years I served as a minister of education in a growing church in the Midwest. Like almost every other church in America at that time, we had a four-part series of classes that we asked members to go through in order to help them understand who we were and what we stood for. One of the classes was devoted to helping members discover their spiritual gifts, and toward that end we distributed a rather well-known spiritual gifts test. Once I began to understand what Paul was really doing in the lists of the gifts, we did away with it and began leading members through a careful consideration of the talents, resources, training, passions, and interests at their disposal. It took longer, but we began to see what Paul intended all along: The Spirit gifts individual believers and churches uniquely, for the purpose of being effective in their own particular cultural context, and to limit the possibilities to only a handful restricts the Spirit's ministry in ways Paul never envisioned.

The Gifts

Now that we have a familiarity with the way Paul's lists work, we can proceed with a discussion of the various gifts that he mentions. Digging into the terminology will help us understand what he's doing and set a rubric for understanding the *kinds* of gifts that the Spirit bestows upon the church for its edification. Organizing the gifts into categories like "miraculous and non-miraculous gifts," or "teaching and non-teaching gifts" will not be helpful, however. Paul never set such a categorization on the gifts, and to superimpose such categories upon them reveals more about our own theology than Paul's.

Above all other gifts Paul esteemed *prophecy* the highest and most

---

5. Fee, *Paul, the Spirit, and the People of God,* 164.

beneficial (1 Cor. 14:1). Some speak of prophecy as if it were merely preaching or exhortation. Paul has other terminology for exhortation or preaching, and "prophecy" distinctly meant speaking an intelligible verbal message through the direct inspiration of the Spirit.[6] New Testament prophecy was akin to the Old Testament variety in that the "prophet" received word directly from God and was expected to deliver the message. Of course, this gift was practically related to the gift of *discernment of spirits*, for the message given had to be corroborated by the testimony of two or three witnesses (Deut. 19:15). Those who had the gift of discerning spirits were coupled with those with the prophetic gift; one delivered the message, the other confirmed whether it was from God (1 Jn. 4:1; 1 Thess. 5:20–21).[7]

Very similar to the gift of prophecy was the gift of *tongues*. More is said about tongues below, but at this point it is helpful to keep in mind that tongues was a gift of speaking in previously unknown but intelligible languages. Luke literally calls it "other tongues" (Acts 2:4) or "languages" (Acts 2:6). Tongues needed interpretation, and as prophecy needed the complement of those who could discern whether the message was from God, so the Spirit gifted others with the *interpretation of tongues* to translate, interpret, and corroborate the message. Without an interpreter, the tongue-speaker edifies only himself (1 Cor. 14:4); the interpreter makes the gift practical and edifies the entire congregation (14:5, 13, 26–28). The gifts of *healing* and *faith* also seem to be coupled in Paul's list in 1 Corinthians 12:9. In this context, faith does not refer to the general faith required of us all for salvation, but rather to the faith to work miracles.[8]

The church needed to understand the message of the gospel, so the Spirit gifted some with *teaching*. Teaching had to do

---

6. Louw and Nida, *Greek-English Lexicon of the New Testament*, 33.449; Turner, *The Holy Spirit and Spiritual Gifts*, 187.
7. E. E. Ellis, "Prophecy in the New Testament Church—and Today," in *Prophetic Vocation in the New Testament and Today*, ed. J. Panagopoulos (Leiden: E. J. Brill, 1977), 52.
8. David Wenham, *Paul: Follower of Jesus or Founder of Christianity?* (Grand Rapids: Eerdmans, 1995), 82.

with instruction in and exposition of Scripture, particularly the Old Testament. Even for Gentile converts, knowing the content of the Old Testament helped ward off attacks from enemies of the gospel. Alongside teaching was *exhortation*, which took the teaching and guided believers into an accepted code of behavior based on that teaching.[9] Exhortation complemented prophecy and teaching in the early church to provide practical means of encouraging believers to live out the faith. There may also be something akin to this "knowledge-insight" coupling in Paul's mention of the gifts of *wisdom* and *knowledge*, but what is exactly meant by these things is still unclear.[10]

Every organization needs clear leadership, so the Spirit gave to some members gifts commensurate with the leadership functions necessary for the health and growth of the church. He gave some the ability to be *apostles*, those men privileged to have seen the risen Christ and to have been personally commissioned by him for specialized ministry. Every believer is called to share the gospel, but the Spirit gifted some to be *evangelists*, those who had extraordinary giftedness (by the Spirit) to spread the gospel message. Some were gifted for *leadership*, the ability to influence others toward a course of action,[11] while others were gifted with *administration*, determining a strategy to get there.[12] Those who devise plans and strategies need foot soldiers to carry them out, so the Spirit endows some with gifts of *service* and *helping*. Still others with an abundance of financial resources at their disposal the Spirit endows with the gift that Paul simply calls *giving*. Paul's only requirement is that those who give do so liberally (Rom. 12:8). Others were given gifts to be specialized

---

9. Georg Braumann, "Exhort, *ktl.*," in *New International Dictionary of New Testament Theology*, ed. Colin Brown 1:567.
10. Bruce, *1 and 2 Corinthians*, 119: "Paul presumably intends some distinction between *sophia* (wisdom) and *gnosis* (knowledge), but the distinction is not clear to us."
11. Louw and Nida, *Greek-English Lexicon of the New Testament*, 36:1.
12. The term we translate "administration" (Gk. *kubernēsis*) appears in early Greek literature as one who steers a ship.

workers of miracles, while others were given the more rudimentary gift of *mercy* (which seems to me the more difficult of the two).

This is the language and vocabulary Paul uses to describe the spiritual gifts. Some of the gifts seem more miraculous, even prestigious, while others seem more mundane. And if we're not careful, we can let those distinctions carry us into the same arrogance that gripped the church in Corinth: a spirit of pride about the more "prestigious" gifts. As we consider the vocabulary, we would do well to remember Paul's counsel that *all* gifts are given for the common good, and that they all come from the same source (1 Cor. 12:4-6).

"I Do Not Want You to Be Ignorant about Spiritual Gifts"

Now that we've considered the gifts individually and considered a brief run-through of the vocabulary involved, it's time to take a step back and think about some of the practical considerations. Having examined the nature of Paul's lists and the vocabulary he used to describe the gifts, what do we learn from Paul?

1. Spiritual gifts are given to be used.

To begin with, the emphasis in Paul's discussion of the spiritual gifts is upon *using* them, not *discovering* them. Paul doesn't spend a lot of time—well, none actually—helping his readers find out what their spiritual gifts are. He doesn't give them litmus tests, psychological profiles, or bubble charts to help them identify their gifts. He operates from the assumption that they all have spiritual gifts and that they are each aware of their giftedness. That doesn't mean that he didn't help them discover the gifts, and it doesn't mean that we are to avoid helping people discover their own gifts. As shepherds of the flock of God we must help the sheep understand how they are gifted. But we cannot allow the discovery of those gifts to outrun or overshadow the fact that the Spirit gave us those gifts to be put to use in his service.

2. The gifts of the Spirit are many.

One thing that naturally flows from the nature of Paul's lists is that there is a plethora of spiritual gifts. To narrow down the list of spiritual gifts to nine or thirteen spiritual gifts (as some do) is incommensurate with the way Paul writes his letters. He mentions a particular set of gifts when writing to the Corinthian church because the situation in Corinth demanded that he mention those gifts and address their abuses. When he wrote to the Romans (from Corinth) he mentioned a very different set of gifts, and those gifts were in large part different from the list he mentioned when writing to the Ephesians. I gather that if Paul had needed to address the topic of spiritual gifts in the book of Colossians, there would be still other gifts mentioned.

All of this suggests that to nail down the gifts of the Spirit to a particular set of nine or thirteen and call them "*the* Spiritual gifts" probably isn't the way Paul viewed the gifting of the Spirit. While music can be learned, some people are spiritually gifted to write songs of worship that edify the body of believers. Paul nowhere mentions music as a spiritual gift, but that doesn't mean that he didn't consider it a gift. It only means he didn't mention it. The gifts of the Spirit are far too numerous for Paul to have given an exhaustive list. It makes me wonder whether spiritual gifts tests that only list nine or thirteen gifts are an accurate way to measure the multitudinous gifts available to the local church.

3. The Spirit gifts each congregation to be effective in its own context.

If the gifts of the Spirit can't be nailed down to a particular set, then how does the Spirit dispense gifts to each congregation? He gifts each congregation to be effective in its own particular context. The church in Corinth was heavy on gifts of knowledge and wisdom, and their misuse of those gifts was unique to that congregation. The church in Rome did not experience those problems (as far as we know) and did not receive from Paul instruction

on the gifts of knowledge, wisdom, speaking in tongues, or discernment of spirits. This suggests that the Spirit had endowed the
Corinthian church with particular gifts and the Roman church
with other gifts. Since they are given for the common good, we
can only conclude that they are given to help the local church be
effective in advancing the kingdom. Just as buildings in suburban
Virginia have a different look than buildings in suburban Orlan-
do, so it is with the church. The gifts at the church's disposal will
look different in rural Kentucky than they will in urban Chicago,
or metropolitan Detroit, or south-central Los Angeles. Each of
those contexts is different, requiring different gifts and ministries.

4. All of our gifts work together for the common good.

Probably the most important aspect of spiritual giftedness
that Paul addresses is the common good for which they are given.
No gift is given for our own personal benefit. Rather, gifts are
given to help the community of faith. No one believer has all of
the spiritual gifts, but each of us has a unique gift or two that is to
be used to build up the church. This means that in every congregation, believers must *work together* to maximize the potential for
which the Spirit gifted us.

This interconnectedness was important to Paul. He prefaced
both of his discussions in Romans and 1 Corinthians with illustrations about the parts of a human body working together to
benefit the whole person (1 Cor. 12:12–26; Rom. 12:4–5). The
emphasis in 1 Corinthians was upon the value of each member
to the body. While one may be a foot and the other a hand, the
hands cannot go where the feet won't take them. We need one
another, and God has combined the various members of the body
in such a way that we have equal concern for one another's well-
being (1 Cor. 12:24–25). The body imagery shows up in Romans,
where Paul declares that "each member belongs to all the others"
(Rom. 12:5). Both of these discussions of spiritual giftedness are
concluded with a discussion of how the gifts ought to be put to

use with authentic love for one another (Rom. 12:9–13; 1 Cor. 13). I have certain gifts, and you have certain gifts. Chances are they aren't the same gifts. So I need you. And you need me. We must not consider our gifts better than the others, but work together in a spirit of love and unity.

What about Speaking in Tongues Today?

Perhaps you're reading this thinking, "Some of the gifts mentioned in the previous section could be categorized as 'miraculous' gifts, like speaking in tongues. Are those gifts still in effect?" I used to have the same question. It's a good one, and you deserve for me to say a few words about the practice of miraculous gifts within the New Testament church. I was raised in, worship in, and teach for a group of churches that has for more than two centuries made it its business to "restore New Testament Christianity." And yet we've never made it a practice to restore the New Testament practices of miracle-working, speaking in tongues, or prophesying. I do not have the space here to write (and you do not have the patience to read!) an exhaustive discussion of the presence or absence of miraculous gifts in the modern church. But I think we can say a few words about the gift of tongues, and let it stand as a representative for the other so-called "miraculous" gifts.

It would be easy to sweep the topic of speaking in tongues under the historical rug, or camouflage it with theological justification for its passing out of existence. Gordon Fee notes that Paul's teaching on tongues (esp. 1 Cor. 14) has become overly important for Pentecostals and an embarrassment for non-Pentecostals.[13] But during Paul's day tongues were fully in effect, and before we proceed with the question of its modern efficacy we must understand its place in Paul's life and in the New Testament.

The first sign of speaking in tongues appears in Acts 2, where

---

13. Gordon Fee, *God's Empowering Presence: The Holy Spirit in the Letters of Paul* (Peabody, MA: Hendrickson, 1994), 10.

the Spirit's initial descent upon the apostles at Pentecost caused
them to speak in "other tongues" (Acts 2:4). The phrase "other tongues" (*heterais glōssais*) denotes other *known* languages, so
each of the foreigners that Luke mentions who came to Jerusalem heard the apostles speaking in his own language or dialect
(Acts 2:6).[14] Several other people are mentioned in the book of
Acts as having received this gift,[15] but ironically Paul is not one
of them. Luke's desire to make Paul the hero of Christ's kingdom
might have been helped by mentioning it. But if Paul's argument
that tongues had become an obstacle to the Gentiles was accurate
(1 Cor. 14:22–25), Luke may have wanted to downplay the practice for his Gentile audience. The concept of "tongues" seems
to have the connotation, at least in Acts, of existing languages
previously unknown to the speaker. Some scholars link praying
in tongues to the "groans that words cannot express" in Romans
8:26.[16] But a close examination of Paul's language denotes that it
is not the believer who utters these inexpressible words, but rather
the Spirit offering them in the presence of God on our behalf, as
our intercessor (Rom. 8:26–27).[17]

By his own admission, Paul spoke in tongues, and apparently
to a greater degree than any in the Corinthian congregation (1 Cor.
14:18). In his long list of instructions to church members on regulat-
ing tongues in the corporate worship service, he poses several hypo-
thetical situations in which he could potentially come and participate in tongue-speaking activity. "If I speak in the tongues of men
and of angels" (1 Cor. 13:1)[18] or "If I come to you and speak in

---

14. And I have no intention of engaging the debate on whether the miracle was on the
    speaker or the hearer.
15. E.g., the household of Cornelius (Acts 10:46) and the disciples of John the Baptist
    (Acts 19:6).
16. Turner, *The Holy Spirit and Spiritual Gifts*, 301; Fee, *God's Empowering Presence*, 575–586.
17. George W. MacRae, "Romans 8:26–27," *Interpretation* 34 (1980): 291–292.
18. Though James D. G. Dunn, *The Theology of Paul the Apostle* (Grand Rapids: Eerd-
    mans, 1986), 438, n. 132 suggests that, because Paul uses the word *alalētos*, "inarticu-
    late," to describe the Spirit's intercession, he probably does not have glossolalia in

tongues" (1 Cor. 14:6) are the kinds of statements that propel his argument forward, but would not have worked had he not spoken in tongues. His argument is not that church members' spirituality is run amok and that they should stop speaking in tongues altogether. His argument is, rather, that they are allowing the ecstatic to get out of control in the corporate worship service, and it is becoming an obstacle to unbelievers. The spirits of the prophets were always under the control of the human prophet, and these believers should likewise exercise control when the Spirit comes upon them. The Spirit will not object, for God is pleased by peace and harmony, not chaos and disorder (1 Cor. 14:33).

So what about speaking in tongues today? Are tongues still in effect? Some of you reading this will be disappointed if I don't unequivocally say "yes." Others of you will be disappointed if I don't dismiss the practice altogether. The question about speaking in tongues is one that everybody wants answers to—either to settle a legitimate curiosity or to pigeon-hole me on one side of the debate or the other. Tongues seem to have been a legitimate expression of prayer in the Pauline churches, even for Paul himself (1 Cor. 14:18). But I have never spoken in tongues. I was raised in the church. My parents took me to church when I was two weeks old, I was baptized at the age of ten, and I can count on one hand the number of Sundays I've been absent from worship. Yet, in all my Christian life, I have never experienced anything remotely related to speaking in tongues. I've not sought it either, for Jesus was quite emphatic that his disciples *not* ask for miraculous signs (Mt. 12:39, 16:4; Lk. 11:29). Some will say that I have not really arrived in the faith. To them, tongue-praying is a mark of spiritual maturity. I am not the one to judge whether or not I am mature. Jesus said, "by their fruit you will recognize them" (Mt. 7:16, 20).

Paul himself, though he prayed in tongues more than any of

---

mind here, since he viewed glossolalia as the language of heaven. He says this contra Fee, *God's Empowering Presence*, 580–585.

the Corinthians, downplayed its use among them and sought to focus their attention on activities more useful to the corporate body. He also emphatically denied that everyone spoke in tongues (1 Cor. 12:30). Jesus never once spoke in tongues, and no man should judge me (or you) less spiritual because I don't. "Each man has his own gift from God; one has this gift, another has that" (1 Cor. 7:7). Tongues were a gift in the first-century church (1 Cor. 12:10), but they are not mine.

■

CHAPTER 9

"As a Father Deals with His Children": Building One Another Up in the Faith

■ MY STUDENTS SOMETIMES GET A CHUCKLE when I tell them that Tom Cruise was not the only German trying to assassinate Hitler.

It's a prelude to the story of the well-known pastor and German anti-Nazi Dietrich Bonhoeffer. He was a bright young boy, born into privilege. His mother was the daughter of Kaiser Wilhelm II's preacher, his father a famous psychiatrist and university professor in Berlin. With this prestigious background, few could have predicted that he would be executed for treason against the German government. A successful pastor and lecturer, Bonhoeffer was gravely concerned about the Third Reich's use of Christian rhetoric to promote its ideology. So Bonhoeffer allied himself with the Confessing Church, a collection of congregations officially opposed to the state church of Germany. He quickly became a leader among them and in 1935 took the position as the president of their seminary in Finkenwalde, training pastors in Scripture, theology, and life.

A colleague once asked Bonhoeffer what he would do if war broke out in Germany. He said, "I shall pray to Christ to give me the power not to take up arms."[1] It wouldn't be long until he was confronted with the reality of the dilemma.

---

1. G. Liebholz, "Memoirs," in *The Cost of Discipleship* by Dietrich Bonhoeffer, trans. R. H. Fuller and Irmgard Booth (New York: Simon and Schuster, 1959), 17.

War did break out in Germany, and Bonhoeffer was forced to take up arms. He involved himself in a plot to assassinate Hitler and, like Tom Cruise's character, Colonel Claus von Stauffenberg in the movie *Valkyrie*, was unsuccessful. Eberhard Bethge, Bonhoeffer's best friend and biographer, would later write that Bonhoeffer in no way believed that everyone should act as he did, but "from where he was standing he could see no possibility of retreat into any sinless, righteous, pious refuge. The sin of respectable people reveals itself in flight from responsibility. He saw that sin falling upon him and he took his stand."[2]

When the assassination plot was discovered, the Gestapo shut down the seminary and intensified the search for anyone connected with the plot. Fearing for Bonhoeffer's life, the leadership of the Confessing Church sent him to New York to escape arrest by the German officials. His friends encouraged him to stay in America and use his gifts as a scholar and theologian. Bonhoeffer found retreat difficult, though, and could not bear to stay while his colleagues and parishioners in the Confessing Church were persecuted for their faith. He stayed in America only two weeks before returning to Finkenwalde. Bonhoeffer's story reveals the heart of a true pastor. He couldn't bear to watch his flock suffer while he lived a life of solace and protection far away. He willingly rushed back into danger to help his people and to see them fulfill the duties of faith and responsibility to the people of God and to the world.

Bonhoeffer's experience is not unlike that of Paul. It wasn't Paul's way to found a congregation and then abandon them, with no involvement in their Christian life. He shared a deep concern for his converts' growth and continued steadfastness in the faith. Like a good shepherd, he cared for, provided for, and protected his sheep.

---

2. J. Doberstein, "Introduction," in *Life Together* by Dietrich Bonhoeffer, trans. J. Doberstein (San Francisco: HarperCollins, 1954), 11.

The Locus of Paul's Authority

Paul wrote, spoke, and behaved as if he had authority over the churches he planted. Scholars have spent the last century attempting to determine his locus of authority, the place from which Paul felt he had the right to direct and discipline these churches. Is it because he founded these churches and believed that they belonged to him, in a sense? Or did he exercise the authority of an apostle, holding the keys of the Gentile kingdom as Peter did for the Jews?

Paul certainly had no problem exercising the authority of an apostle. Scholars are divided over exactly how far Paul used his apostolic authority to motivate his congregations, and I don't want to engage the debate here. Some believe that his rights as the "thirteenth apostle" gave him leadership control over the Gentile churches, while others are quick to point out that the term "apostle" has more than one meaning in the New Testament. Paul certainly used his apostleship to his own advantage (1 Cor. 9:1; 2 Cor. 12:11). He almost always identified himself as an apostle in his writing, believed he had the right to be paid for his work and to take a believing wife just like the Twelve (1 Cor. 9:5), and challenged the would-be "super-apostles" in Corinth about whether their apostleship matched up to the example that he set in his own ministry (2 Cor. 11:5–15). He believed that he was no less an apostle than Peter, and challenged Peter as a peer in areas where Peter was mistaken (Gal. 2:8–9, 11–14).

While Paul felt comfortable using his commission as an apostle to defend his ministry (and that's really what the previous examples demonstrate), the authority he exercised in the churches for spiritual growth was more akin to that of a parent rather than an apostle. Sometimes he compared himself to a mother tenderly caring for her children (1 Thess. 2:7), feeding them with spiritual milk (1 Cor. 3:1–3), and laboring in childbirth until Christ is formed in them (Gal. 4:19). Other times he compared himself to a father (1 Thess. 2:11) who gave affection to his children (2 Cor. 6:13), warning them as a father would (1 Cor. 4:14). He thought of converts like Timothy (1 Cor. 4:17; 1 Tim. 1:2, 18; 2 Tim. 1:2, 2:1; Phil. 2:22), Titus

(Tit. 1:4), and Onesimus (Phm. 10) as his "sons." Paul became the father of the Corinthians in the face of their "ten thousand guardians" (1 Cor. 4:15), and his irritation with their problems stemmed not from his authority as an apostle, but from his love and care for them as their spiritual "father." The term "father" was frequently used to denote a spiritual teacher, whose disciples were his "children."[3] In this way Paul called upon his readers to imitate his example, not just because he gave birth to these people and churches, but because he was their spiritual teacher in a real master-apprentice kind of way.[4]

Shepherding by Proxy

Shepherding the churches under his care was made all the more difficult for Paul because of his itinerant ministry of evangelism. Paul was constantly on the go, moving from town to town in order to spread the gospel throughout the Roman Empire. His *modus operandi* was to begin in the synagogues, then preach to the Gentiles, and stay in one place as long as he could. Sometimes he got to stay for as long as eighteen months (in Corinth) or up to three years (in Ephesus). But other times Paul faced persecution rather quickly and had to leave town. Thessalonica is a good example. Paul preached in the synagogue there for three weeks, then turned to the Gentiles, and in short order was run out of town (Acts 17:5–10). Because they were his genuine converts, Paul felt an intense connection with the Thessalonian church. He called them his joy and crown and intensely longed to see them again (1 Thess. 2:17–20). Caring for them so, he wanted to see them grow and reach maturity in Christ. How would he have been able to do so after being banned from the city?

---

3. For instance, in the wisdom literature of the Old Testament Solomon assumes the role of the teacher and continually calls the reader "my son": Prov. 1:8, 10, 15; 2:1; 3:1, 11, 21; 4:10, 20; 5:1, 20; 6:1, 3, 20; 7:1; 19:27; 23:15, 19, 26; 24:13, 21; 27:11; 31:2; Eccl. 12:12. Peter called John Mark his "son," though no scholar assumes they were related (1 Peter 5:13).

4. Interestingly enough, he never used the parenting imagery to call upon his personal imitation in the Epistles to the Romans and the Colossians. He was not the founding father of these churches.

One of the ways Paul continued to shepherd his converts was by sending *surrogate shepherds* to disciple them. When he was run out of Thessalonica, he left Timothy and Silas behind in nearby Berea to shepherd the church in Thessalonica in his absence (1 Thess. 3:2). In doing so, the men he sent in his stead developed their own affections for the churches. Titus had a great affection for the Corinthians (2 Cor. 7:6-7, 13-16, 8:16-24) and for the churches on Crete (Titus 1:5).[5] As we discussed in chapter four, these men were well-schooled in Paul's philosophy of ministry and were sent in his stead because he had confidence that they would represent him well.

Another method Paul used to his advantage in shepherding the churches came through his *letter-writing*. There was no postal service willing to deliver Paul's letters, so they were often sent in the hands of a surrogate. Letters like those we find in the New Testament weren't written to be read with the eyes, but rather designed to be read aloud[6] to the entire congregation. They were a written form of rhetoric and would have been performed publicly, in a sense, before the intended audience. There are several clues and hints of this in Paul's letters, even the ones addressed to individuals.[7] Writing letters allowed Paul to address the entire church and demonstrate what Michael Gorman calls "apostleship in absentia."[8] Paul used his letters to give thanks for his converts and their faith, to criticize them for their wrongdoings, to encourage them to live better, and to give them instructions about further action. There is also evidence that

5. Eusebius, *History of the Church*, 3.4.6 tells us that Titus, after his ministry in Dalmatia (2 Tim. 4:10) went to Crete and became the bishop over the churches until he died.

6. See Witherington, *The Paul Quest*, 93.

7. Paul sometimes dictated his letters to an amanuensis (i.e., secretary or scribe) like Tertius (Rom. 16:22) or perhaps Luke (2 Tim. 4:11). In several instances the scribe was unnamed (cf. 1 Cor. 16:21; Gal. 6:11; Col. 4:18; 2 Thess. 3:17), but that Paul wrote a greeting in his own hand indicates that someone else was writing down the letter as Paul dictated it, or even "preached" it (as it were). The letters were to be read aloud in the churches (1 Thess. 5:27; Col. 4:16), and even the ones addressed to individuals like Timothy bear marks of a corporate audience. Paul concludes 1 Timothy by saying "Grace to you all" (6:21, personal translation).

8. Gorman, *Apostle of the Crucified Lord*, 74-75.

letters in a particular geographical area were shared by churches, for he instructed those in Colossae to swap letters with the believers in Laodicea (Col. 4:16). Writing letters allowed Paul to shepherd congregations from a distance, for the letter brought Paul and his authority near, effecting a more ready response from his readers.[9]

Nothing compared, however, with the face-to-face interaction and personal discipleship that Paul was so good at. So when he had finished an evangelistic tour, he made plans to go back through that area "strengthening the churches" (Acts 15:41). Once he had gone through the region of southern Galatia and eastern Asia Minor planting churches, he intentionally retraced his steps through those areas, touching base with the churches to ensure their faithfulness (Acts 14:21-24). His next journey began by going through the Galatian churches a third time before he proceeded into western Asia Minor and into Greece (Acts 16:1-5). On his third journey he went through Galatia once more, strengthening the churches there before he set on to revisit the churches in Asia Minor and Greece that he previously founded (Acts 18:23). Paul was the "founding father"[10] of these churches, and his love for them transcended his presence.

Portrait of a Biblical Shepherd

As a faithful, Scripture-thumping Jew, Paul was well-acquainted with the stories about the shepherds of God's people in the Old Testament. God's original intent for the priesthood was to reveal God to the people and to intercede between them and God as Moses did on Mt. Sinai. But the priests abandoned their God-given duties about as quickly as the people fashioned the golden calf, and

---

9. That the letter was regarded as a surrogate for the person himself can be seen in a letter from Seneca to Lucilius: "I thank you for writing to me so often; for you are revealing your real self to me in the only way you can." Quoted in Stanley Stowers, *Letter Writing in Greco-Roman Antiquity*, Library of Early Christianity, ed. Wayne A. Meeks (Philadelphia: Westminster, 1986), 29. Additional references to letters carrying the real presence of the writer can be found in Stowers, 38-39, 62, 65.

10. Ernest Best, "Paul's Apostolic Authority—?" in *Journal for the Study of the New Testament* 9 (1986): 17-18.

by the time we get to the Babylonian exile the prophets were delivering oracles against the shepherds of Israel. These shepherds had become lazy and insolent; they had failed to erect the proper fences to keep the sheep from wandering, and they could not protect the sheep from predators (Isa. 56:9–12; Ezek. 34:1–10; Jer. 23:1–2). In each of these oracles God promised to remove them and provide Israel with one good shepherd (Ezek. 34:23; Jer. 23:4–6). When Jesus stood and proclaimed, "I am the good shepherd" (Jn. 10:11, 14), he declared that he was the promised Shepherd of Israel (cf. 1 Peter 5:4). Paul imitated Jesus in providing loving care for the flock over which he had been entrusted. The things he found the shepherds of Israel neglecting in the prophetic oracles were the things that he made sure to provide for his flock.

So he fed them. He taught them the basic precepts of the faith. He stayed in Corinth for eighteen months teaching them the word of God (Acts 18:11) and in Ephesus for three years. The church in Antioch was his "home church," and when he wasn't on the road, he stayed there, teaching the people (Acts 13:1, 14:28, 15:35). He continually implored his readers to hold fast to his teaching (1 Cor. 11:2; 1 Thess. 4:1–2; 2 Thess. 2:15, 3:6, 14), for he knew it would eventually make them complete in Christ (Col. 1:28). Any good shepherd knows that lambs need milk until they're ready for solid food. When they were ready, he fed them deeper things, sometimes in response to their own questions on such matters as the living having advantages over the dead in the afterlife (1 Thess. 4:13–18), or the second coming (2 Thess. 2:1–12), or the Lord's Supper (1 Cor. 11:17–34), or marriage (1 Cor. 7), or spiritual gifts (1 Cor. 12). Paul led his sheep to green pastures (Ps. 23:2) where they could eat and be satisfied.

Paul also erected fences. Sunday School books and children's Bibles tell us sheep are cuddly and cute, but the reality is that sheep are quite dumb. They are like the cattle I grew up around. Never content with the grass in the field, they constantly push against the fence, stretching for the greener grass on the other side. They need boundaries, or they wander off into the wilderness (Lk. 15:4). Paul, like any good shepherd, let his sheep know where the boundaries were and kept them in. The prime example here is the man in Corinth who had gone to bed with his father's new wife (1 Cor. 5:1-2). This lay outside the boundaries of the holiness and honor of the church, and Paul spared no words shaming the participants and the congregation (who used the situation to boast about how "free" they were in Christ) back into the pen. The Corinthian congregation had many questions about exactly where the boundaries were in relation to marriage (ch. 7), meat publicly sacrificed to idols (ch. 8), the proper use of spiritual gifts in the assembly (chs. 12-14), the resurrection of the dead (ch. 15), and about the collection of monetary gifts for the Jerusalem church (ch. 16). Paul was happy to help them understand exactly where the boundaries were set.

Shepherds don't put up fences just to keep the sheep in. They put them up to keep predators out, and Paul's churches faced several predators—"savage wolves," as he called them (Acts 20:29-30). The Galatians were oppressed by a group of Christians who demanded compliance with Jewish customs (especially food laws, circumcision, Sabbath-keeping, and special feast days) in order to inherit the salvation of the Jewish messiah. Paul wrote his most passionate letter to the Galatians to defend them against these predators, calling their philosophy a completely different gospel (Gal. 1:6), and one that ought to be shunned. Predators like Hymenaeus (1 Tim. 1:20; 2 Tim. 2:17), Alexander (1 Tim. 1:20; 2 Tim. 4:14-15), Philetus (2 Tim. 2:17), Elymas (Acts 13:6-12), believers who refused to work in Thessalonica (2 Thess. 3:6), and the "super-apostles" plaguing the Corinthian church (2 Cor. 11:1-15, 12:11-13) were enemies of the gospel and needed to be opposed. Sheep can't defend themselves and often become easy targets for malicious beasts. Knowing this, Paul cared enough about his congregations to step over the fence and protect them from the enemies of the gospel.

It wasn't just his own churches he cared about either. Paul showed a demonstrated concern for believers across the world, even in cities and areas where he hadn't planted churches. Paul longed to have a ministry in Rome (Rom. 1:10, 15; 15:23–24), and wrote the letter to the church in Colossae, a church planted by Epaphras (Col. 1:6–7), instructing them about Christian maturity. And when he met with the apostles in Jerusalem, laying out for them the gospel he preached to the Gentiles, they added nothing to his message, but one condition: that he remember the "poor" (Gal. 2:10). "The poor" seems to have been a euphemism for Jewish Christians living in Jerusalem. In addition to physical persecution at the hands of the Jews, the Jewish Christians in Jerusalem often faced economic hardship, giving them the label "the poor." The apostles simply wanted to remind Paul that, in his zeal to preach the gospel to the Gentiles, he should not forsake the ministry to the Jews, as Jesus had instructed (Mt. 10:5–6). Paul was eager to comply. His concern for those in Jerusalem was an extension of the concern he shared for the entire people of God. These were not ultimately his sheep, but belonged to the Chief Shepherd, and if he could help any of them grow he was willing, whether he planted the church or not.

"I Would That All God's People Were Shepherds"

Perhaps you're thinking, "Well, that's a fine lesson on the business of shepherding God's people. But I'm not a pastor. How does this help *me* walk in the Spirit?"

The reality is, Paul expected normal people without ministry degrees to assist local elders and pastors in the work of shepherding the flock. The Colossians were to "teach and admonish one another" from the Word which dwelt in them (Col. 3:16). He told the Thessalonians to "warn those who are idle, encourage the timid, help the weak, be patient with everyone" (1 Thess. 5:14). Though he'd never met them, he believed that members of the church at Rome were "competent to instruct one another" (Rom. 15:14). While God had given some to be ministers and shepherds (Eph. 4:11), Paul very much believed that each person who had been indwelt with the Spirit of God was able to become a conduit through whom the Spirit could do the work of conviction and encouragement.

The concept that we're speaking of is what the Reformers called "the priesthood of all believers." One of the problems that they noticed in the church was the tendency for the priests to do all the work of ministry. The Reformers began to see that the New Testament called every believer a priest. Peter said to his readers, "You are . . . a royal priesthood" (1 Peter 2:9). God's intention all along was for Israel to be an entire kingdom of priests (Exod. 19:6). Yes, the Spirit gifts us all differently and gives us different tasks to perform within the people of God (Rom. 12:4–8; 1 Cor. 12:12–31). But the fact that he gifts us differently doesn't negate the fact that he gifts *all* of us to serve.

Joshua once tried to get Moses to make two unauthorized prophets stop speaking. Moses, knowing they had the Spirit of God on them, simply said, "I wish that all the LORD's people were prophets and that the LORD would put his Spirit on them!" (Num. 11:29). Peter declared at Pentecost that the Spirit is been poured out on all of God's people (Acts 2:38–39). If you are in Christ, you too have the Spirit of God. If you're concerned that doing the work of a shepherd may usurp your pastor's role, I'd simply say that any pastor worth his salt is going to agree with Moses: "I wish that all the Lord's people were shepherds."

Strays

Sheep don't always stay inside the pen, though. They often find sweet-smelling grass on the wrong side of the fence, and having found it, wander off alone, way outside the protection afforded by the shepherd. What do we do when that happens? Do we recognize that all people have free will and are free to walk away from the faith, and thus we let them go? This was one of the criticisms leveled against the shepherds of Israel—their failure to go after the lost and the strays (Ezek. 34:4). There's a time to let them go, but that's not the first step. Jesus, following the oracle of Ezekiel, said that we should go after them (Lk. 15:4; Ezek. 34:16).

I work in an environment where young people, training for ministry, are trying to do the right thing. They come to us expecting God to reveal himself in a clear way about their purpose in his kingdom, and they genuinely desire to follow him. But they come to us from a variety of backgrounds. Some arrive with a well-developed Christian background, extensive exposure to the church, and their spiritual discipline already worked out. Others come to us with no church background, and don't have much of a clue what living the Christian life means. With them, our work is nearest to the heart of Pauline gospelizing—teaching them about Jesus and how he wants them to live. There is a third group that comes to us with a modicum of Christian background. They know they are to live a holy lifestyle that honors Christ, but haven't had any opportunity or any challenge to put it to practice and work it out on a daily basis. I began my work here with the expectation that young people training for ministry would be of the highest ethical quality. Many have lived up to that reputation. But I've had to sober my expectations with the reality that leaders fail (both young and old), that leaders are still human, and that "We all, like sheep, have gone astray" (Isa. 53:6). If you spend any time in the local church, you'll find people you love and care about wandering outside the fences into dangerous territory.

So what do we do when that happens? Do we go after them? And if so, what does that look like in real life? Every situation will be different, so there's no cookie-cutter formula for this kind of thing. But let me suggest a few things I see in Paul.

Work from an "inclusive" standpoint

One thing I note from Paul's example is that Paul never considered someone "outside the flock" when they strayed. The Corinthian man's sexual misconduct was about as serious a sin as the ancient world saw. Paul characterized it as a sin that even the pagans wouldn't commit (1 Cor. 5:1). Paul had some very harsh words for this man about his conduct and for the Corinthian church for allowing it to continue. But his rhetoric never sprang from this man's excommunication from the church. Paul considered him still a member of the flock of God's people, and his harsh words arose from a platform of calling to live a lifestyle in conjunction with his membership. Paul still hoped for this man's restoration.

I remember in high school reading Jonathan Edwards' sermon *Sinners in the Hands of an Angry God*, in which he depicted God dangling us over the pit of hell by a spider wire, ready to drop us in any time we sin.[11] I thought this was old-school theology and was shocked when I entered ministry to find people still thinking of God this way. Paul, on the other hand, knew that we live in between the time when we've been saved and the time when we'll be fully made whole (1 Cor. 13:9-12). In the meantime, we fail. That doesn't mean that high standards aren't to be expected or that we shouldn't try to live a righteous life. Neither does it mean that we get to weed people out of the kingdom who we think ought not to be there (Mt. 13:28-30). Paul never disciplined a person by threatening them with exclusion from the promises of God until they've had ample time to repent and then willingly refused.

Work toward repentance

Another thing I see in Paul's example is his desire for wayward sinners to repent. God is nuts about repentance (Ps. 51:17; Lk. 15:7, 10, 22-24), and Paul's corralling of stray sheep always had repentance in mind. Discipline was included, to be sure. He handed over Hymenaeus and Alexander to Satan, but for the express purpose

---

11. Edwards remarked that as "it is easy for us to cut or singe a slender thread that any thing hangs by: thus easy is it for God, when he pleases, to cast his enemies down to hell." In *Jonathan Edwards: Basic Writings*, ed. O. E. Winslow (New York: The New American Library, Inc., 1966), 152. Though, this is something of a caricature of Edwards' theology.

that they might "be taught not to blaspheme" (1 Tim. 1:20). He asked the Corinthian church to put out the sinful man, but only until such time as he repented and his sin destroyed (1 Cor. 5:4–5). It's disconcerting to our modern rights of privacy that Paul had no qualms naming some of these people, calling them out publicly. Some of their names are recorded for all of history in the pages of Scripture. But doing so was right in line with social conventions of letters of blame,[12] and Paul always had the subject's repentance in mind. Paul didn't view discipline as a wholly bad thing, but a necessary part of shepherding his people. After all, the rod and the staff, they comfort (Ps. 23:4).

If you find yourself dealing with a wayward believer, wondering what to do about it, let me encourage you, in the tradition of Paul and Jesus, to work as best you can toward their repentance. There must be confrontation of sin; that may involve you alone, or it may mean getting other people involved (Mt. 18:15–20). The best way to elicit repentance, though, is not judgment, and certainly is not by calling their salvation into question. Rather, often the best way to go is by calling them to understand the offense that their sin brings to Christ and his people. Remind them of the offense, and then remind them of God's kindness. Paul believed that God's kindness is what ultimately evokes our repentance (Rom. 2:4).

> Dealing definitively with sin is God's business, and God's way of dealing with the sin business is forgiveness. This does not mean that moral intentionality and effort is useless or inappropriate on the way, only that sin as a thing-in-itself is beyond our power to get rid of whether within ourselves or in the people or institutions for which we have

---

12. See Stowers, *Letter Writing in Greco-Roman Antiquity*, 51, 85–87, 133–134, 139–141; Witherington, *The Paul Quest*, 115–118.

> responsibility. In dealing with sin we don't do it on our own, we deal with God as he deals with sin. Dealing with the intricacies, the subtleties, and the pervasiveness of sin requires God in his mercy. And the overall way that he does it is to forgive.[13]

Searching after wayward sheep and bringing them back into the fold is hardly ever more complicated than this. Emotionally difficult? Yes. More prolonged and anguished at times? Definitely. But hardly ever more complicated. It's as simple as Jesus said it was: one believer showing another believer his fault, and leading him to repentance and restoration. And I think it's by God's design that it be that easy. You don't need a theology degree or a ministry license to shepherd your fellow believers into Christian maturity. The Spirit of God is already at work in each of us toward this goal. And it's not just about discipline. It involves a whole host of activities that result in the feeding and caring of God's people. Whether it's feeding them resources to grow, answering questions they may have about the Scriptures, praying together, holding them accountable for something they struggle with, or more blatantly calling them out on sin, the process is still easy enough. Every believer can help shepherd the flock as Paul did.

---

13. Eugene Peterson, *The Jesus Way*, 99.

■

CHAPTER 10

"The Marks of Jesus":
Paul and Suffering

■ THERE ARE A LOT OF THINGS THAT BAFFLE the godly. As we try to understand God's ways and apply them to the world, issues begin to surface for which we simply don't have answers. And sometimes the answers we *do* have don't satisfy us or even make sense. What happens to the soul of an infant who dies prematurely? Why did God tell Saul and his men to kill the Amalekites—men, women, and *children* (1 Sam. 15:1-3)? Where was Jesus *really* during those three days in the tomb? The twentieth-century monk Thomas Merton once said that it was "the very nature of the Bible to affront, perplex and astonish the human mind. Hence the reader who opens the Bible must be prepared for disorientation, confusion, incomprehension, perhaps outrage."[1] Theologians in every era of Christian history have tried to systematize the faith and boil it down to a palatable slice, yet some things still elude understanding. And nothing is more elusive or confounds the integrity of the mind like human suffering.

The problem of suffering isn't a modern conundrum, for Christian history is filled with literature attempting to make sense of the problem. Good men and women, extremely intelligent and

---

1. Thomas Merton, *Opening the Bible* (Collegeville, MN: The Liturgical Press, [1970], 1986), 11.

highly respectable, have taken their shot at working out the problem of reconciling human suffering and God's sovereignty, and
probably the two most notable are Philip Yancey's *Disappointment
with God* and C. S. Lewis' *The Problem of Pain*.

But to be honest, sometimes the answers traditionally given
have left me unsatisfied and perplexed. I remember the first
time I read Jean Pierre de Caussade's *The Sacrament of the Present Moment*—a spiritual classic that counsels us to attend with
wholehearted devotion to whatever God has anointed for us in
the moment—the only quote I seemed to be able to remember
had to do with God *dragging* the soul through seasons of suffering to produce vibrant faith in his people.[2]

Of course, Scripture teaches us that "suffering produces perseverance" in us, as well as character and hope in God (Rom. 5:3-4),
and sometimes God disciplines those he loves (Heb. 12:4-11). But
does God really *drag* us through suffering just to produce faith in us?
Is all the suffering that we encounter a matter of discipline for sin?

My grandfather taught me so. When I was about twelve years
old, a series of tornados ravaged the small, central-Kentucky town
where we lived and blew over a large oak tree, crushing his farm
truck. As we stood in the driveway awaiting the insurance agent to
come and take pictures, my grandfather said, "I guess the Lord is
disciplining me for something I did wrong. Now I just gotta figure
out what it is." It sounded pious to me, and I was too ignorant of
biblical history to know that it wasn't biblical. Whenever God *did*
discipline his people, he always gave them several opportunities
to repent beforehand and *never* disciplined them without telling
them exactly why!

The belief that suffering is the result of sin is as old as the Gospels themselves. Jesus's disciples once asked him if a man's blind-

---

2. Jean-Pierre de Caussade, *The Sacrament of the Present Moment*, trans. Kitty Muggeridge
   (San Francisco: HarperCollins, 1989), 22. "However mysterious it may seem, it is
   in order to awaken and maintain this living faith that God drags the soul through
   tumultuous floods of so much suffering, trouble, perplexity, weariness and ruin."

ness was the result of his own sin or that of his parents. Jesus's only response was (if I may loosely paraphrase), "Neither. Watch this!" (Jn. 9:1-5). To be fair, *some* suffering may result as a consequence of my sin. But to speak of *all* suffering as the result of sin runs counter to Jesus's own viewpoint and sounds contrived to non-believers. Tsunamis are caused by the shift in tectonic plates in the ocean floor, and to date no amount of human disobedience has been able to influence them. As helpful as it is to explain suffering in terms of the result of human sinfulness, it doesn't explain everything.

It has also become fashionable in some circles to explain human suffering in terms of God's kingdom advancement. You'll sometimes hear statements like, "God allowed this to happen for his glory and his purpose," or "God wants to *use* this tragedy for good." Perhaps you've even said them a time or two. These kinds of statements reflect Paul's comments (though completely out of context) that "in all things God works for the good of those who love him" (Rom. 8:28). Never mind that Paul was not speaking of the tragedy of human suffering here; comments like those described above suggest that God uses humans as pawns in some sadistic program of kingdom advancement.

These two explanations of suffering—sin and kingdom advancement—usually manifest themselves most readily in the face of tragedy. Kevin Roose spent a semester studying (undercover) at Liberty University, and notes that these two themes comprised most of the on-campus rhetoric—in prayers and sermons—in response to the Virginia Tech shootings in 2007.[3] God was either punishing immorality on the university campuses of America, or orchestrating this situation in order to maneuver someone to the forefront who could speak kindly about him. The rhetoric of sin and kingdom advancement. None of this

---

3. Kevin Roose, *The Unlikely Disciple: A Sinner's Semester at America's Holiest University* (New York: Grand Central Publishing, 2009), 234-238.

was novel or original. The same rhetoric appeared in school assemblies at Columbine, in political comments after Katrina, and in churches after 9/11. Find human tragedy and you'll likely find the rhetoric of sin and heavenly conquest.

This discussion of suffering is absolutely integral to our study of Paul precisely because suffering was prominent in his life. Acts and the Epistles are filled with references to his suffering, from his being beaten and left for dead in Lystra (Acts 14:19), to his boasting of his "weakness" (2 Cor. 11:23-33), to his defense to the Galatians that he bore on his body the *stigmata* ("marks") of Jesus (Gal. 6:17). Paul's suffering was an integral part of his life, but must be set in the proper perspective.

There is a tendency to consider Paul's suffering a matter of God's punishment for his pre-conversion persecution of the church. God specifically told Ananias, "I will show him [Paul] how much he must suffer for my name" (Acts 9:16). But to consider Paul's suffering as retribution for his previous way of life makes God seem capricious and vindictive, and furthermore, doesn't fit the point that Luke has been driving throughout Luke and Acts: anyone who wants to truly follow Jesus must be prepared to suffer as Jesus did.[4] In many cases Paul suffers because he is *doing* God's will, not because he is *disobeying* it. Neither was Paul's suffering a way for God to maneuver him into greater preaching of the gospel. Paul's suffering often means

---

4. Those who follow Jesus must be prepared to take up the cross, forfeit their own lives, and "taste death" for the kingdom (Lk. 9:23-27). He cautioned them to always pray (Lk. 18:1; see Spencer and Spencer, *The Prayer Life of Jesus*, 42-45). To a man who professes unswerving allegiance to him Jesus says, "the Son of Man has no place to lay his head" (Lk. 9:58), precisely because he has just been rejected in Samaria. Disciples of Jesus must be prepared for this kind of rejection. Peter and John were thrown in prison and threatened (Acts 4:3,21) as representatives of the early church, and then widespread persecution broke out against the church (Acts 8:1). Luke continually drives home the early church's identification with the death of Jesus and typifies its climax in the death of Stephen (Acts 7:54-8:1).

that he's run out of town and *prevented* from doing any more ministry in that location.[5]

Oddly enough, when we come to the life and ministry of Paul, though we find a man who was willing to suffer, and did quite often, we are hard-pressed to find him *explaining* his suffering. Paul accepts his suffering as a part of his partnership with Christ, but did not feel the need to explain its presence in his life to his readers. He wasn't concerned about answering the question, "Why does a loving God let me suffer this way?" He willingly offered his life—and death—to Christ Jesus as thanksgiving for the suffering Christ underwent for Paul's salvation.

We have noted earlier that Paul may have seen himself as the counterpart to the Suffering Servant of Isaiah 42–56. As Jesus suffered for the sins of the world, Paul may have viewed himself as Jesus's partner, a Robin to Jesus's Batman, completing the story. I do not mean by this that Jesus had left anything undone at Calvary, or that his work of redemption was deficient in any way. But to explain what I *do* mean, it's probably best to turn now to a short exposition of the Song of the Suffering Servant in order to set the stage rightly. Once that's done, we will note how prominently Paul's view of Jesus as the Suffering Servant appears in Paul's preaching and Epistles, and then move to a consideration of Paul's ministry as a drink offering poured out alongside the Lamb (2 Tim. 4:6).

The Song of the Suffering Servant

The Song[6] of the Suffering Servant is the story of Israel's way-

---

5. Immediately after his conversion Paul began preaching in Jerusalem, but the antagonism of the Jews caused him an early departure (Acts 9:29–30). His near-death experience in Lystra caused him to have to give up ministry there (Acts 14:19–20), and the rioting of the crowds caused his early departure from Thessalonica (Acts 17:5–10) and Ephesus (Acts 19:23–20:1).

6. I recognize that many scholars will hasten to point out that they see several servant "songs" in the text of Isaiah. I have no intention of engaging the debate about the strophes within the text, or even the debate about the unity of the book of Isaiah.

ward heart, God's graciousness, and the willingness of the Servant to bear the punishment for Israel's sins. Scholarship is quite
divided on who the Servant represents to Isaiah. Some believe the
Servant to be the nation of Israel, others Cyrus the Persian king.[7]
The Ethiopian eunuch's question to Philip—"who is the prophet
talking about, himself or someone else?" (Acts 8:34)—suggests "a
predisposition towards an individual,"[8] and it seems that is how
the New Testament writers understood it.

The song begins with the story of Israel's disobedience. God
had laid out a plan for Israel's faithfulness and she had disregard-
ed it. His people took oaths but did not fulfill them (Isa. 48:1),
and as a mule's neck is "stiff" when it refuses to be led by a rope,
so Israel's neck was stuff as iron to Yahweh's guidance (48:4).
Wrath had become an impending doom upon Israel and God,
in his mercy, had delayed it for another time and purpose (48:9).

That time and purpose needs to be seen in conjunction with
the introduction of the Servant into the song. God had foreseen
(literally, I mean) Israel's plight and had previously introduced
the Servant into the mix. "Here is my servant, whom I uphold,
my chosen one in whom I delight; I will put my Spirit on him
and he will bring justice to the nations" (Isa. 42:1). The first part
of Isaiah 42:1 could be translated, "my servant whom I love, in
whom I am well pleased," and anyone familiar with the Gospels will recognize this as the formulaic saying resounding from
heaven at Jesus's baptism (Mt. 3:17; cf. Mk. 1:11; Lk. 3:22). The
Servant is now re-introduced as one who was made for this spe-

---

The major purpose for our discussion here is the overarching theme of the Suffering Servant as Paul knew it in the text of Isaiah in his day.

7. For a survey of the history of interpretations surrounding the Servant, both Jewish
and Christian, see Christopher R. North, *The Suffering Servant in Deutero-Isaiah:
An Historical and Critical Study* (Oxford: University Press, 1948). For a concise presentation of the Servant as an individual see Oswald T. Allis, *The Unity of Isaiah*
(Philadelphia: Presbyterian and Reformed, 1974), 81–101.

8. Sydney H. T. Page, "The Suffering Servant between the Testaments," *New Testament Studies* 31 (1985): 490.

cial purpose from birth, and the one in whom God's glory would be revealed (Isa. 49:1–3).

The Servant's purpose and mission is to willingly bear what "is in the Lord's hand" (49:4), and we come to find out later that what is in the Lord's hand is a cup of blood-colored wine (51:17–23). Symbolically, in the song, it represents the wrath that is due Israel for her disobedience. The Lord takes the cup out of the hand of his people and promises they will never drink from it again (51:22). The visual images in the song work like this: Israel holds the cup of wrath she has brought on herself, Yahweh declares his intention to remove it from her hand, and the Servant knows that what is in the Lord's hand is appointed to him. In other words, God has appointed the suffering to be removed from Israel and passed on to a substitute in her place.

Enduring this suffering will require the Servant's complete and utter obedience, and many lines in the Song describe just how difficult this will be. The Servant refuses rebellion against his lot and offers his back willingly to those who beat him (50:6). When his tormentors want to pull out his beard (shameful for a Jew), he does not hide his face (50:6). Like a hardened flint stone against which metal is sharpened, he has set his face resolutely for this suffering, for he knows that ultimately he will not be put to shame (50:7). These same themes appear in the most famous lines of the song (53:3–7) as the Servant is despised and rejected, pierced, crushed, and inflicted with punishment. He is completely and utterly obedient, for as sheep are quiet before their shearers, so he did not open his mouth in protest to Yahweh's wishes (53:7).

As a result of the Servant's obedience, two things will happen (and this is where we begin to find themes that will ultimately connect us to Paul's outlook on suffering). *First, the Servant will be vindicated.* God will not let the Servant's obedient suffering go unanswered. He knows that, though it seems dire now, he will *not* be shamed (50:7) and "after the suffering of his soul, he will see the light of life" (53:11). In a world where the continuation of the bloodlines was immensely important, Isaiah describes the Servant's vindication in terms of offspring: "though the LORD makes his life a guilt offering, he will see his offspring and prolong his days" (53:10). Because the Servant is obedient to the suffering appointed him, Yahweh numbers him among the great (53:12) and describes him in the kinds of exalted terms that are reserved for God in the Old Testament: "raised and lifted up and highly exalted."[9]

Second, as a result of the Servant's work, *salvation will be offered to the entire world—Jews and Gentiles alike.* Isaiah describes the Servant's work as accomplishing salvation for Israel, but then quickly turns to God's further intentions: "It is too small a thing for you to . . . restore the tribes of Jacob and bring back those of Israel I have kept. I will also make you a light for the Gentiles" (Isa. 49:6). Once that salvation comes, God will "beckon to the Gentiles" and lift up his banner to the "peoples" (49:22). Foreigners and eunuchs will have a welcome place in the kingdom and offer sacrifices alongside "all nations" (i.e., Gentiles; 56:3-8). Justice is promised, not just to Israel, but to the nations (42:1; 51:5; 52:10, 15) and the distant islands (49:1; 51:5).

This is the Song of the Suffering Servant, in its broadest thematic content, as it appears in Isaiah 42-56. It's a story of the disobedience of God's people and the gracious means by which God provided for their (our) disobedience to be punished and while also offering an opportunity for release, redemption, freedom, and salvation. It's the story of God's offer of salvation to his own people, and then to the Gentiles. The people rejoice in this news, for he exclaims, "How beautiful on the mountains are the feet of those who bring good news, who proclaim peace . . . salvation, who say . . . 'Your God reigns!'" (Isa. 52:7).

Jesus, Paul, and the Suffering Servant
It's easy to see, then, how the New Testament authors saw Je-

---

9. John N. Oswalt, *Isaiah Chapters 40-66* (Grand Rapids: Eerdmans, 1998), 378.

sus's life and ministry against the backdrop of the Suffering Servant Song of Isaiah. Jesus is found in the Gospels saying that he
must go to Jerusalem and *must* suffer a horrendous death (Mk. 8:31;
Lk. 22:37, 24:19-23, 24:44-47; cf. Mt. 17:22-23; Mk. 10:33; Lk.
18:31-33). He speaks of his suffering as that which brings deliverance for the people, both as a ransom (Mk. 10:45) and as a mother
hen bearing the brunt of a barnyard fire as she hunkers over her
chicks (Mt. 23:37-39). They live as she suffers their judgment.[10]
Three times he asks the Father, "Let this cup pass from me" (Mt.
26:39, 42, 44). Jesus was well-versed in the scroll of Isaiah,[11] and the
background seems to be the cup of suffering that had been taken
out of Israel's hands, was now in the hand of the Father, and was
appointed to the Servant. Time and time again the Gospels present
Jesus as the Suffering Servant promised in Isaiah.[12]

Paul also believed that Jesus was the Suffering Servant, for several times he explicitly connects quotes from the Suffering Servant
Song to his presentation of Jesus. In the synagogue in Thessalonica
Paul reasoned with them from the Scriptures that it was *necessary*
for the Messiah to suffer and *then* enter his glory (Acts 17:3). He
wrote to the Corinthians, "God made him who had no sin to be a
sin offering for us" (2 Cor. 5:21), a statement that is reminiscent of
the themes found in the Song about the innocent suffering for the
guilty (Isa. 53:9-10). The lofty Christ-hymn in Philippians 2:6-11
bears those themes as well, as the one who was exalted in the begin-

---

10. N. T. Wright, *Jesus and the Victory of God* (Minneapolis: Fortress Press, 1996), 570-571.
11. Direct quotes from Isaiah appear on Jesus's lips in Mt. 13:14-15; 15:7-9; 21:13;
    Mk. 4:12; 7:6-7; 9:48; 11:17; 13:24-25; Lk. 4:17-19; 8:10; 19:46; 22:37; Jn. 6:45.
12. Explicit references are found in Mt. 8:16-17, 12:15-21; Lk. 22:37. The Synoptics
    paint John the Baptist's ministry against the one in Isaiah 40:3 who comes to "pre-
    pare the way for the LORD" (Mt. 3:3; Mk. 1:2-3; Lk. 3:4-6; Jn. 1:23). Jesus then comes
    on the scene as the Servant who follows in his steps (Isa. 42:1-4; Mk. 1:4-9). At
    Jesus's baptism the voice from heaven says, "This is my Son, whom I love; with him
    I am well pleased" (Mt. 3:17; Mk. 1:11; Lk. 3:22). These words are a direct quotation
    from Isaiah 42:1 regarding the Servant. It seems obvious that they are pointing us
    in the direction of Jesus being the Servant of Isaiah. If so, readers can anticipate the
    coming suffering and vindication found in the larger scope of the Servant Song.

ning with the Father leaves his lofty place, suffers willingly, and is
then exalted to the highest place in vindication for his obedience.
This small sampling of texts (and more could be offered) surely
shows that Paul believed Jesus had more than a passing connection
with the Song of the Suffering Servant.

One of the results of the Servant's obedience, we noted, was
the offering of God's salvation to the Gentiles. But when you
consider that Jesus ascended back to heaven before the gospel was
officially offered to the Gentiles, and that Paul considered himself
the apostle to the Gentiles, this question arises: Could Paul have
seen himself as the counterpart, or the official agent, of Jesus Messiah to complete that task? Witherington sums this up well:

> Could Paul, following in Christ's footsteps and
> seeing himself as Christ's agent, have seen him-
> self as the servant of Isaiah, and for this reason
> seen himself as called upon to spread the light
> among the Gentile nations? Paul knew that
> Christ during his own life had basically been un-
> able to carry out such a task. But Christ could get
> the job done through his agent or ambassador
> Paul. Does this also explain why Paul talks about
> filling up the sufferings of Christ or sharing his
> sufferings (cf. Phil. 3:10)?[13]

While I would not go so far as to say that Paul identified himself with the Servant *per se*, Paul certainly describes his ministry in
terms of ideas and themes that come from the Suffering Servant
Song. He wants Gentiles to call upon Christ Jesus for salvation
and membership in the covenant community, and Paul hopes to
offer them as a fragrant offering to Christ at his return (Rom.
15:16). But they cannot call upon the Christ they've never heard

---

13. Witherington, *The Paul Quest*, 172.

of; and they won't hear of him unless Paul preaches; and he cannot preach unless he is sent out. But when he is sent out and preaches and they call upon Christ, they will exclaim with Isaiah, "How beautiful on the mountains are the feet of those who bring good news" (Isa. 52:7; Rom. 10:15).

Paul saw Jesus as the Suffering Servant of Isaiah, and likely saw himself as the ambassador, the agent, the herald, and partner of the Suffering Servant in order to flesh out the fulfillment of the prophecies in Isaiah that he believed were fulfilled in Jesus.[14] He wanted to fill up in his flesh that which was lacking in regard to Christ's afflictions (Col. 1:24) and then present the Gentiles to Christ as a fragrant offering at his return (Rom. 15:16; Isa. 66:20). Now that we have this in mind, it becomes easier to understand why Paul suffers for Jesus with such pride, and why he suggests that those who are allied with Jesus must also be prepared to do so. The story that Isaiah tells is one of salvation offered to the world from the context of suffering. Paul now works to bring that salvation to the world, just as Isaiah had foretold.

Paul and Suffering

Paul's entire Christian life was bound up with suffering. In fact, from the time of Paul's conversion God was speaking of Paul's life as one of suffering. He told Ananias, "I will show him how much he must suffer for my name" (Acts 9:16). It's common to see Paul's suffering as justice for his persecution of the church in his pre-conversion days, as if God had said, "Because Paul made my people suffer, I will make him suffer." But if we note that the statement about suffering falls quickly on the heels of Paul being the chosen instrument to take the gospel to the Gentiles (Acts 9:15) then we have a bit more perspective. Paul was called to finish God's plan which

---

14. See Köstenberger and O'Brien, *Salvation to the Ends of the Earth*, 148, 165–166, 170. "Paul is not suggesting that he was the new servant of the Lord. Rather, his mission arises from and, in a sense, is a continuance of that of the Servant who had been set apart by the Lord from birth with a specific ministry to Gentiles in view" (166).

began with the Servant and still involved salvation in the midst of suffering. In other words, Paul was called to finish the story. And the story is imbued with suffering.

And Paul willingly bore it. Both Acts and the Epistles are filled with accounts of his suffering, from the plots and abusive talk of his Jewish opponents (Acts 13:45; 14:2; 18:6) to their eventual action (Acts 13:49–50; 21:27–30). From the very beginning of his Christian life, Paul was rejected by other Christians who didn't trust him (Acts 9:26). Consider the things Paul faced as an apostle of Christ: floggings (Acts 16:23; 2 Cor. 11:23–24; a near-miss in Acts 22:25), beatings (1 Cor. 4:11; 2 Cor. 6:5, 9; 11:25), imprisonments (Acts 16:23–24; 24:23; 28:16, 30; 2 Cor. 11:23; Eph. 6:20; Col. 4:10; Phil. 1:7, 12–18; Phm. 9, 13; 2 Tim. 1:8), riots (Acts 17:5–9; 19:23–41; 2 Cor. 6:5), and plots to kill him (Acts 14:5; 20:3; 23:12). Paul was frequently stoned (Acts 14:19; 2 Cor. 11:25), run out of town (Acts 14:5–6; 1 Thess. 2:15), dragged before the authorities (Acts 18:12–13), shipwrecked (Acts 27:27–44; 2 Cor. 11:25), hungry (1 Cor. 4:11; 2 Cor. 6:5; 11:27; Phil. 4:12), sleepless (2 Cor. 6:5; 11:27), naked[15] (1 Cor. 4:11; 2 Cor. 11:27), despised (Acts 17:32; 1 Cor. 4:11; 2 Cor. 6:8), and under the constant threat of death (Rom. 8:36; 1 Cor. 4:9; 2 Cor. 1:8–11).

But what is more astounding than the litany of trouble Paul faced in spreading the gospel was his willingness to embrace it as an ambassador of Christ. When the prophet Agabus predicted that Paul would be bound in Jerusalem, Paul's ready response was, "I am ready not only to be bound, but also to die in Jerusalem for the name of the Lord Jesus" (Acts 21:13). He was proud of the "marks" (*stigmata*) that he bore on his body, probably referring to the scars that he had acquired from the above-mentioned persecutions (Gal. 6:17). He delighted in persecution (2 Cor. 12:10) and

---

15. In the sense that he did not have the *proper* clothing, either for the season or for social etiquette.

hoped to become like Christ in his death, and then (like Jesus) be vindicated in resurrection (Phil. 3:10–11).

Paul was willing, even proud, to suffer these things for his Lord. But why? Why was he so willing to undergo these hardships just to preach the gospel? The way is narrow, but surely not *that* narrow! A few texts from Paul's letters suggest that he saw these sufferings as inevitable as the Servant's servant. If Jesus suffered to bring salvation to the Jews and make God's righteousness available to the Gentiles, then Paul would have naturally seen his own ministry in actually making the *offer* to the Gentiles in tandem with Jesus's sufferings. "The sufferings of Christ flow over into our lives," he told the Corinthians (2 Cor. 1:5), so much so that "we always carry around in our body the death of Jesus" (2 Cor. 4:10). He expected suffering to be so much a part of his existence that he continually told the Thessalonians that he and his companions would be persecuted (1 Thess. 3:4). Was it because he had some insight into an upcoming situation, some prophecy the Lord had given him about a specific persecution anointed for him? Perhaps. But if Paul really did count himself as the companion of the Suffering Servant, then the expectation of suffering in connection with the offering of salvation to the Gentiles fits perfectly within his understanding of Jewish scripture. Paul saw his sufferings as "filling up" or completing the sufferings of Christ in his (Paul's) own flesh for the sake of his (Jesus's) body—the church (Col. 1:24).

Like a modern concert or symphony, I have been holding back the main event until the end, attempting to build to a grand crescendo. Without question the one text that most clearly reveals Paul's self-image as partner of the Suffering Servant is a statement he made at the very end of his life. Languishing in a Roman prison, knowing that he would not be released (as he had been in Acts 28:30–31), Paul said in his last written letter, "I am already being poured out like a drink offering, and the time has come for my departure" (2 Tim. 4:6). The drink offering is no mere obligatory toast to Paul's life, but is drawn from the Old Testament requirements for the priestly sacrifices. Twice daily the priests sacrificed a lamb, along with an offering of grain and wine (Exod. 29:40–41; Num. 28:7). Paul is careful *not* to say that he is being slaughtered like a sacrificial lamb, for in his messianic theology, the Lamb had already been slain. But he characterizes his own life as a drink offering, *consistently and daily poured out alongside the Lamb.*

If the Suffering Servant Song really does lie behind Paul's understanding of his sufferings, then it's easy to see why vindication language sometimes appears in connection with his description of his trials. Immediately after characterizing his life as a drink offering, he says that the crown of righteousness awaits him (2 Tim. 4:8). His confidence that the Lord will rescue him from every evil attack and bring him safely into his kingdom (2 Tim. 4:18) falls on the heels of a statement about being rescued from the mouth of lions (2 Tim. 4:17). Some suggest that Paul had fought the wild lions in the coliseum at Ephesus,[16] but he may be alluding to Psalm 22, where David pictures his own suffering akin to being placed in the mouth of roaring lions (Ps. 22:13), then pleads with God, "Rescue me from the mouth of the lions" (Ps. 22:21). Psalm 22, like many of David's psalms, is a story of persecution, faithfulness, and vindication for the righteous sufferer,[17] a theme noted earlier as part of the major conclusion of Isaiah's Suffering Servant Song. If Paul saw himself as Jesus's counterpart, then he likely saw Psalm 22—on Jesus's lips during the crucifixion—as an expression of his own anguish and hope, meditating on it in his final hours just as Jesus did.

---

16. First Corinthians 15:32: "If I fought wild beasts in Ephesus for merely human reasons, what have I gained?" Did Paul actually fight wild beasts, or is he speaking figuratively? For a short survey of interpretations on both sides see Robert E. Osborne, "Paul and the Wild Beasts," *Journal of Biblical Literature* 85, no. 2 (1966): 225–230.

17. In *The Spirituality of Jesus*, 60–61, I state: "Psalms 22 and 31 reflect a larger pattern of suffering and vindication in David's psalms, suggesting that Jesus may not have felt so abandoned. The context of both psalms is Yahweh's vindication of the innocent David, who trusts in him. Jesus may have been citing the Psalms in expectation of deliverance rather than crying out in agony."

Suffering and the Jesus-Kind of Life

Not only was Paul willing to bear this suffering for Jesus, he taught his readers that those who allied themselves with Jesus Messiah must also be prepared to suffer. He told Timothy that "everyone who wants to live a godly life in Christ Jesus will be persecuted" (2 Tim. 3:12). To be allied with a suffering Messiah naturally brings opposition in a world that is still in the process of being redeemed. And for Paul, it was simply part of the Jesus-kind of life. If those who follow Jesus must be prepared to take up the cross and follow him, then for Paul it was more than preparation. It was an ever-present reality.

The extent to which suffering extended into Paul's view of the Christian life can be seen in an enigmatic series of statements he made in 2 Timothy 2:3–7. He begins by counseling Timothy, "Endure hardship with us like a good soldier of Christ Jesus" (v. 3). He reinforces that devotion with three illustrations, involving a soldier, an athlete, and a farmer. He gives no interpretation, but instead instructs Timothy to reflect on his illustrations and pray that the Lord give him insight. At first glance they are confusing, and if we're not careful to apply them to the overarching statement "endure hardship," we will miss what Paul is saying.

"No one serving as a soldier gets involved in civilian affairs—he wants to please his commanding officer" (2 Tim. 2:4). Every soldier knows that his basic training—yea, his very existence—will be one of hardship. Timothy is to keep his focus on pleasing his commanding officer, no matter how difficult, and keep himself from becoming entangled in non-kingdom affairs. "Similarly, if anyone competes as an athlete, he does not receive the victor's crown unless he competes according to the rules" (2 Tim. 2:5), that is, competes lawfully. One of the "laws" or rules that Jesus laid down is that following him very often involves suffering.[18] And finally,

---

18. Followers of Jesus must be prepared to "take up the cross" (Mt. 10:38–39, 16:24–28; Mk. 8:34–9:1; Lk. 9:23–27) and endure rejection when spreading the message

"The hard-working farmer should be the first to receive a share of the crops" (2 Tim. 2:6). Timothy is farming righteousness, and with it comes a reaping of trouble and persecution. If Timothy is farming righteousness and the gospel, with persecution and hardship as a natural byproduct, then he must be willing to taste the "firstfruits" of that crop.[19]

The possibility of suffering for the cause of Christ is more an everyday threat in other countries than it currently is in the United States. Sure, politicians are always labeled as potential antichrists, and there will never be any shortage of those who want to convince us that modern lawmakers are passing legislation to persecute Christians in one way or another. But outright persecution is not the norm for us here in the United States as it is in other countries, and as it was for Paul and his churches. He regularly taught his converts that trials were to be expected, prepared for, and endured patiently, for "you know quite well that we were destined for them" (1 Thess. 3:3).

So we're "destined" for these trials? Is Paul talking only about himself and his traveling companions? Or does he mean us too? Am I "appointed" to suffer for Jesus? And if so, what does that say about the character of God? These are serious questions, and perhaps we should spend some time with them before we conclude.

Does God Want Me to Suffer?

Paul suffered a great deal, and willingly, in honor and devotion to his Lord Jesus. He seems to have identified himself as the co-agent of Isaiah's Suffering Servant, whose suffering brought atonement to Israel and the inclusion of the Gentiles into the people of God. He taught that those who allied themselves with Christ were

---

(Mt. 10:14–23, 24:9–13; Mk. 13:9–13; Lk. 10:10–16; 21:12–19). Jesus frequently told his followers that persecution and trouble would follow them as they followed him (Lk. 12:11–12, 49–53; Jn. 16:33, 17:14, 21:18–19), but also pronounced blessings upon those who endured it for his sake (Mt. 5:10–12; Lk. 6:22–23).

19. For deeper insight into this line of thinking see Knight, *The Pastoral Epistles*, 392–396.

bound to suffer with him and prepared his converts for that very real possibility. All of this talk about Paul's suffering, and his teaching on suffering, naturally leads to some pesky questions. Does God want me to suffer? Has he appointed suffering for me? It certainly seems so, from some of the Scriptures we've considered so far.

But these statements must be balanced with other statements Paul made that hint in the other direction. Timothy was to lead the congregation in prayer for kings and authority figures "that we may live peaceful and quiet lives in all godliness and holiness" (1 Tim. 2:2). Paul gave the same instruction to Titus, that the people be obedient to the rulers and be peaceful (Titus 3:1–2), presumably with the same goal of quiet living. Given that Paul experienced so much opposition, his statements likely reflect his hope that the congregations of these two apprentices will live under the radar of the empire, in peace and quiet, without the threat of persecution or tribulation.

Two extremes must be balanced in this discussion as we try to accurately weigh the evidence. On the one hand, God wants good things for his people. We cannot run this too far into the health-and-wealth, "God, bless me with vitality and money" gospel (which is really no gospel at all). On the other hand, we must be prepared to endure suffering for the cause of Christ. We follow a man who willingly laid down his life for the salvation of the world. Jesus predicted that if suffering came to him, it would come to his disciples, and then reminded them, "A student is not above his teacher, nor a servant above his master" (Mt. 10:24; cf. Mt. 24:9).

How do I put them together? In this way: God wants good things for me, and intends to bless me. It is not his desire to crush me and cause me to suffer. But suffering will inevitably come, and he also wants me to love him so much, to be devoted to his son Jesus so much, that no amount of suffering will deter my devotion. This is what I see in Paul, and it seems to make the most sense of Paul's statements about God supplying all the needs of his hearers (Phil. 4:19), while simultaneously preparing them for the very real possibility of suffering in the name of Jesus (Phil. 1:27–30).

Two very important things need to be said in conclusion about suffering and the way of Christ. The first involves the *manner* in which I suffer. We could argue all day long about whether God ordains suffering or allows it, and indeed theologians in Christian history have expended gallons of ink doing just that. I have no interest in determining whether or not God causes our sufferings. Paul never considered that his sufferings were caused by God, but were rather enacted by "evil men" (2 Thess. 3:2), "bandits" (2 Cor. 11:26), impostors (2 Tim. 3:13), his own countrymen (i.e., Jews or Jewish Christians, 2 Cor. 11:26), and even Satan (1 Thess. 2:18).

The work of spiritual formation is about the heart-related questions, and my *response* to suffering displays the extent to which I am conformed to the image of Christ. When I suffer, do I curse my persecutors or do I pray for their forgiveness (Mt. 5:43–48)? Do I respond to suffering with ill will toward the Father, or do I pray for strength to endure it, as Christ did? Does my suffering cause me to pray for more boldness to proclaim the message, or do I shrink back into the safety of silence and withdrawal? Sometimes the question of my *response* to suffering is of more concern to the Father and to my own spiritual development than is the question of its *origin*.

Finally, this point deserves reiterating: The Scriptures—from the Psalms, to the Suffering Servant song, to Paul, to Revelation—continually overwhelm us with the promise of vindication for the righteous sufferer. Those who suffer in obedience to the Father, as Christ did, receive blessing and vindication, as Christ did. It may or may not be in this lifetime, but the promise of vindication occupies a conspicuous place in God's world and his scheme of redemption. Those who suffer for him can rest *assured*—not merely hopeful—that no amount of suffering on Christ's behalf will go unnoticed by him. "He has not despised or disdained the suffering of the afflicted one" (Ps. 22:24) and will give to those who cry out under his altar white robes and the promise that, in his own time, he will give an opportunity for repentance to their tormentors and cause the mountains to fall on those who refuse it (Rev. 6:9–17).

Jesus's suffering was God-ordained from the time of Isaiah (even from the fall; Gen. 3:15), and while he struggled with it, he was ultimately obedient to the Father, who then vindicated him for that obedience in resurrection. His suffering was connected to the salvation of the nations, and so it was also for Paul, whose life-ministry to offer God's salvation to the Gentiles could not be divorced from his own suffering. "Believers take on a suffering particular to them that is positively connected to God's redeeming humanity and all creation from suffering."[20] Rather than thinking about suffering as a result of sin or God's capricious plan for savage amusement, perhaps we should take our cues from Paul and consider that whatever suffering (if any) we endure because of the gospel is a necessary step toward the redemption of the lost.

---

20. L. Ann Jervis, *At the Heart of the Gospel: Suffering in the Earliest Christian Message* (Grand Rapids: Eerdmans, 2007), 8.

■

CHAPTER II

The Shape of Pauline Spirituality

■ WE'VE SPENT THE LAST SEVERAL CHAPTERS combing through the Scriptures to find evidence of Paul's routine spirituality, the ways that he partnered with the Spirit in everyday living. We found Paul to be a man of prayer, praying constantly for his converts and for new opportunities to preach. We found Paul preaching the gospel, hailing Jesus as the uncontested Lord of the universe. Paul was willing to suffer for Christ, and he considered his tribulation a necessary complement to Christ's afflictions. He constantly trained co-workers, fellow evangelists, and ministers to carry on his work and guard the faith past his lifetime. He regularly worshiped with God's people, in both the synagogue and the church. He read Scripture honestly and faithfully, and continually pointed his converts, both Jew and Gentile, to its pages to answer questions about their newfound salvation in Christ Jesus. Paul expected his converts to live lives of holiness, and he set a good example, subjecting his flesh to righteousness and boasting of a clean conscience before the Father. Paul cared for his churches and his converts and continued to provide them with guidance and direction in his absence. And he put his spiritual gifts to use in a godly and faithful way to build up the church, as he expected every believer to do. These are the tools of righteousness that cultivated the seeds of grace and spirituality in his letters and his life.

But now it's time to take a step back from the trees and have a look at the forest. There's always a danger in an examination of this type to get so locked into the study of the details that we miss the larger picture. So in this chapter I want to spend some time putting the whole package together. Paul encouraged his readers to imitate him, to watch him live life in the Spirit, and then to follow him as he followed Jesus. But what does that look like? If we follow Paul and seek to live the Christian life in ways that are in line with him, what is included? What is *not* included? Does that mean that we imitate him in every last detail? If not, then what can we reasonably exclude? What aspects of his spirituality were common to and even necessary for first-century Christian living, but not fitting for the twenty-first century? These are the kinds of questions that occupy our attention in the pages that follow.

The Shape of Pauline Spirituality

Now that we've come to the end, it's time to think about what an authentic Pauline spirituality looks like. There are six components to it that I would like to explore as relates to Paul's spirituality, and how it works in the modern world.

Faithful to Scripture

Go to any local bookstore and check out the spirituality section and you'll find two things: 1) spirituality is really in vogue these days, and 2) not much of it is rooted in the Judeo-Christian Bible. "Spirituality" has become a catch-word in our world for "whatever makes me feel like I'm in touch with the divine." As such, it's highly subjective, with no foundation in objectivity whatsoever. A generation ago Ray Bradbury wrote *Fahrenheit 451* and made the Bible a central prop in the story—a book that was in danger of being erased from the pages of history. These days the story is more likely to be the one reflected in *The Book of Eli*, where the Bible is still jealously guarded as a holy text, but ultimately shelved alongside many sacred texts—one option among many. The new spiritualists of our day love Jesus, and they love to quote the Bible. But they nearly always do so out of context, twisting the meaning and the direction, the *mise en scène* of the text.

Any practice of the Spirit that is genuinely Pauline will be authentically biblical. Paul was committed to Scripture—to its words, its meaning, its direction, and the goal toward which Scripture was pointing. He quoted a lot of Scripture, but never took it out of context. His citations, allusions, and arguments from Scripture were faithful to the text and to what the original authors intended to convey through their writings.

There is a kind of "biblical" that is inauthentic, that uses the Bible to bully and to justify. It is the kind of "biblical" that hammers infidels over the head with proof-texts, prunes verses from the vine in order to justify personal plans and desires, and scours the text for clues that substantiate end-time theologies. Eugene Peterson describes it as a kind of reading that only seeks to satisfy our Holy Wants, Holy Needs, and Holy Feelings.[1] Paul didn't treat the Bible that way. Instead, he let Scripture *form* him, transforming his desires into those of God. Only then were his citations of text authentic and genuine.

Rather than using the text as a magic book of personal fulfillment, a field manual for heretic warfare, or a hidden code to decipher the time of the second coming, we would do well to see the Bible as a tutor leading us to godliness through Christ. As I read the stories contained in it, I'm led to consider, "How would I have responded? Is this about me? Does this reflect something in my own life?" The stories of Israel's rebellion make me wonder what sinfulness lies in the depths of my own heart. The Sermon on the Mount makes me realize that God has a different idea for the way he wants me to live my life. As I read Matthew 23, I'm reminded that it's quite possible for the most religious people in the world to miss what God is up to. And if I ever needed guidance on how to talk to non-believers about Christ, I simply turn to Acts 17 and watch Paul flip pagan philosophy up on its head and demonstrate that the way of Christ is the "good life" (Acts 17:22–31; 1 Tim.

---

1. Peterson, *Eat This Book*, 31-35.

6:17–19). The text guides us, leads us, corrects us, trains us, re-
bukes us, and prepares us to be people of God ready to do every
good work Christ calls us to (2 Tim. 3:16–17).

Imitates Jesus

As Paul worked out the Spirit of God in his life, his primary
example was Jesus. While Paul saw Jesus as the Lord of the universe, in whom "all the fullness of the Deity dwells" (Col. 2:9
NASB), he also viewed him as our brother, as intensely human.
Jesus was filled with the Spirit, and while his practice of the Spirit
included casting out demons, walking on water, healing, and raising the dead, he also *grew* in the Spirit (Lk. 2:40, 52), working
out the implications of living in the Spirit in daily routines. Paul
found in Jesus a paradigm of what the Spirit-filled life looks like.

So he imitated Jesus. Jesus prayed, with intense prayers that
were both honest and respectful before the Father (Heb. 5:7). So
did Paul. Jesus identified potential candidates among his followers and trained them for further ministry. So did Paul. Jesus spent
time with God's people in worship and there found opportunities
to let the Spirit speak, either through his preaching or through
the Scriptures. So did Paul. Jesus went throughout the towns and
villages of his world, preaching and teaching the good news of
the kingdom of God. So did Paul. Jesus did not play favorites and
welcomed into his company the sinner and the saint, the tax collector and the teacher of the Law, the foul and the Pharisee. So
did Paul. Jesus also gave his life in service to the Father, knowing
that if he was obedient he would be vindicated. So did Paul. As
Paul fleshed out the everyday workings of the Spirit, he looked to
Jesus as an example. His call to us is not simply, "Imitate me," but
rather, "Imitate me *as I imitate Christ*" (1 Cor. 11:1).

As soon as we say, "Imitate Jesus," we are immediately confronted
with a very serious question: "How far?" To ask the question, "What
would Jesus do?" is much more difficult in practice than it seems.
Do we imitate Jesus in his dress? Must we live where he lived and

eat the food he ate? Must we learn Aramaic and keep kosher? Must we begin preaching in Jerusalem and only when we're done there branch out into Judea, Samaria, and the ends of the earth (Acts 1:8)? These are questions that must be asked, and when we come down to it, most of us will answer those questions with a resounding "No!" Which leads me to the next facet of Pauline spirituality.

Founded in Freedom

Jesus is the standard, and those who follow in his steps must walk the *way* that he walked, live the *way* that he lived. No one has ever walked the way of Christ with more integrity than Paul. But not even Paul believed that he was to imitate Jesus in every last detail of his life. Jesus primarily preached in the synagogues in Galilee. Paul didn't. Jesus walked on water. Paul didn't. Jesus regularly cast out demons as a sign that the kingdom of God had arrived. Paul didn't. Jesus's primary message was, "The kingdom of God is near," or better translated, "The kingdom of God *has arrived*" (Mk. 1:15). Oddly enough, the phrase "the kingdom of God" isn't that frequent in Paul's letters. And while I suppose that every time Jesus opened his mouth it could be counted as prophecy or the oracles of heaven, there's no record that Jesus ever spoke in tongues or prophesied as Paul did.

Even in his language Paul didn't imitate Jesus exactly. Jesus's favorite phrase for himself was "Son of man," and it perplexes me as a student of the New Testament that Paul never used this phrase to refer to Jesus. Instead, Paul said *new* things about Jesus. He called him "Lord" and carefully worked out what that meant to both Jewish and Gentile listeners. Jesus had no problem using the phrase *egō eimi* ("I Am"), the very name of God revealed in Exodus 3:14, to refer to himself. Paul is careful not to use that language, for when he said to Timothy, "Christ Jesus came into the world to save sinners, the worst of whom I am" (1 Tim. 1:15, personal translation), he inverted the words (*eimi egō*)—he was careful not to imitate Jesus in that way. He would not imitate Jesus in calling himself by the name of the Father. At the end, he compared his life to a drink offering being poured out *alongside* the Lamb (Exod. 29:40-41; 2 Tim. 4:6). He would not refer to himself as the lamb—only the drink offering. In his theology, the Lamb had already been sacrificed.

Authentic Pauline spirituality is not about imitating Jesus *exactly*, in every single little detail of his life. Rather, authentic, Paul-style practice of the Spirit is founded in freedom. "It is for freedom that Christ has set us free" (Gal. 5:1). While Jesus had no systematic, organized plan for offering the gospel to the Gentiles, Paul saw that Israel's Scriptures foretold the time when it would happen and was commissioned by God (with the Spirit's help and approval) to get it done. Paul was constantly adapting his strategy to help people understand the gospel (1 Cor. 9:22). He was free to describe the work of Jesus, not in terms of a mother hen dying to protect her chicks, as Jesus did (Mt. 23:37-38), but rather as a reconciliation of two estranged parties (2 Cor. 5:18-20), as the fulfillment and conclusion of the Law (Col. 2:14; Gal. 3:23-25), as the "wisdom" of God (1 Cor. 2:6-16), as the "good news" (i.e., "gospel") come to the empire, and as the "fullness" of all things (Col. 1:15-20). Jesus never wrote anything, while Paul found the freedom to write letters, preserving his ideas about Jesus for all eternity. Our world sees the way of Jesus as restrictive, oppressive, and full of guilt. Paul's preaching, his life, and his methodology all point to the freedom that Christ wrought for the people of God through his death. In his methodology, his language, and his spirituality, Paul found the freedom to work for the promotion of the message, goals, ideals, integrity, and lordship of Jesus in ways that were most effective for his own culture.

This suggests that, even in Jesus-style living, there is great freedom. Freedom from guilt and perfection, yes. But so much more. Freedom to honor Christ in new ways. Freedom to proclaim him through new media. Freedom to write new songs and poems about him. Freedom to explore new ideas about him through the Scriptures. Freedom to draw new portraits of him, to write new novels about Christians who live with integrity and honor, and to make movies which honor the ideals for which he stood. In short, freedom to glorify Christ.

Glorifies Jesus

Freedom comes with boundaries, though. I'm free to drive anywhere I want, provided I stay on public roads and off private property. So it is with our Christian freedom. I'm free to explore new avenues in Christ, to map out new territory for his kingdom. But this freedom is not license to do anything and everything I want. There are boundaries—fences that must be erected to keep my territory-marking honorable. That fence, that boundary, is the glorification of Jesus. Anything that doesn't glorify Jesus is out of bounds.

"Glory" was on Jesus's mind right up until the very end of his earthly life. On the night he was betrayed he prayed that the next few hours of his life would glorify the Father (Jn. 17:1–5). John portrays him as "the glory of the One and Only" (Jn. 1:14), and yet Jesus's concern was not his own glorification, but the glorification of the Father. In a very down-to-earth way, to "glorify" God means *to make him look good*. It means to represent him in such a way that he gets a good reputation among those who either don't know him or are skeptical. Peter described Christian living this way when he wrote, "Live such good lives among the pagans that, though they accuse you of doing wrong, they may see your good deeds and glorify God" (1 Peter 2:12). While I hear Eugene Peterson protesting in the background, "We're not in charge of publicity for the Almighty,"[2] there is something in the way we live our lives that either turns people on to the person of Christ or turns them off. To glorify Jesus means to enhance his reputation in a positive way. This is the boundary to our freedom.

Authentic Pauline spirituality always seeks the best for Christ,

---

2. Peterson, *The Wisdom of Each Other*, 80.

his kingdom, and his reputation. I find Paul doing whatever he can to increase the reputation of Christ in the Roman Empire, even at the expense of his own reputation. Paul is willing to suffer, to be degraded, to be run out town, to be chained up like a petty thug, to endure the scorn of his countrymen, to go hungry and thirsty, and to live on the bare necessities of life, all in the hopes that every person who comes into contact with him will see Jesus in a positive light.

Paul's life is a challenge to us, a continuous caution to play inside the fence. Our tendency is to look out for our own best interests instead of the well-being of those around us. We want a good reputation for ourselves, a good name for our career, and if Jesus looks good in the process, well good for him! We're not naturally accustomed or culturally conditioned to begin with the question, "What would make Jesus look good in this situation?" When we read the pages of Acts and the Epistles, we find in Paul a man who was willing to put the glorification of Jesus—Jesus's reputation, Jesus's name's sake, Jesus's work—above every other thing in his own life, even if it meant destroying his own reputation in the process. Paul's life demonstrates a concern for Jesus's well-being and reputation ahead of his own. That's what it means to glorify Jesus.

Committed to Unity

I grew up in a collection of churches known as the Stone-Campbell Movement or the "Restoration Movement" (i.e., Christian Churches/Churches of Christ). The movement originally began as a plea for unity. One of the pinnacle events in our early history was the Cane Ridge Revival (1801), a joint effort by Baptist, Presbyterian, and Methodist ministers who threw off their creeds and preached the simple truth found in the Scriptures. The revival was a major event in early American church history, and though it occurred less than fifteen miles from my childhood home, I had no idea of its implications until I went to college and studied the history of our movement. Most students of Restoration history come to revere Thomas Campbell, who withdrew from the Presbyterian Church because of its sectarianism. (Campbell—as a minister in the Old Light, Anti-Burgher, Seceder Presbyterian Church—was not permitted to offer communion to Presbyterians of any other sect, not even the *New* Light, Anti-Burgher, Seceder group.) These early American believers were committed to the unity of the church. They threw off the creeds and divisive theologies that separated believers from one another and embraced the simple gospel. They took seriously Jesus's prayer "that all of them may be one" (Jn. 17:21).

Becoming spiritual, like Paul, will mean committing to work toward the unity of the body of Christ. Paul was ardently concerned about Jews and Gentiles getting along and finding a common salvation in Christ. He worked hard to make sure neither Jew nor Greek, neither rich nor poor, neither slave nor free was ostracized in any way in a local church. He worked hard to curb abuses within the local churches which separated believers from one another.

Practically speaking, I think this amounts to two things. On a personal level, it rules out any notion of a privatized religion in the name of Jesus. Paul did not come to institute a religion of self-improvement, and his letters were not written to lead me to personal and individual salvation. They weren't even meant to be *read* individually, but rather *out loud* before the entire congregation. An authentic Pauline spirituality is committed to the entire *body* of Christ.

On a corporate level, though, it also means that we must become more focused on *unity* of the church at large. Our world—like Paul's world, like Thomas Campbell's world—is full of Christian divisiveness. Church splits, worship wars, and petty feuds still plague the church today as they did then. Theological infighting—Christian groups arguing and fighting about their own personal theologies, casting dissenters as heretics and "false teachers"— do not enhance Jesus's reputation in positive ways. These conversations have to be had, for they help both parties see the other side of the coin. But we must be careful to have them in ways that are God-honoring, and in the humility, the sacrifice, and the integrity of Christ Jesus.

Unity is not to be sought at all costs, though. Even the Stone-Campbell Movement has its dark history of liberalism. In the early twentieth century, a branch of the movement began to take the Bible less literally, treating it as myth and fable. In the eyes of many within the movement, this branch watered down the gospel, went soft on the Scriptures, and introduced foreign innovations into New Testament Christianity that early church history called heresy. Unity cannot be sought at the expense of truth. Paul would have no unity with men like Hymenaeus, Alexander, Phygelus, or Hermogenes until they had repented of their errors and embraced the truth. Truth, as found in the Scriptures, is the common ground for the church, and where we all find commitment to God-revealed Scriptural truth, even at the expense of our own presuppositions, we find the seedlings of unity.

Spirit-ual

Finally, and by no means least importantly, an authentic Pauline spirituality is just that—*Spirit*-uality. It is characterized by life in the Spirit of God. Jesus, after receiving the Spirit in baptism, went into Galilee preaching the good news of the kingdom and working miracles by the power of the Spirit. While I don't have the ability to do the miracles that he did, I do have the ability to walk in the power of the Spirit as Jesus did. Though Paul spoke in tongues, prophesied, and saw visions of heaven, he didn't do as many miracles as Jesus did. He still claimed that he had the Spirit of God, though, and that leads me to this conclusion: walking in the Spirit isn't automatically bound up with the miraculous.

As I watch the Spirit of God work throughout the book of Acts, I find that his work is very earthy, *mundane* in the classic sense of the word (from the Latin *mundanus*, "of the earth"). Sure, he shows up with great fanfare, causing the Apostles to speak in tongues. But once he's on the scene, he works in very quiet ways. The seven deacons were chosen because they were "full of the Spirit" (Acts 6:3), and for them, walking with him meant distributing food and caring for widows in the church. When the Spirit directed Philip to speak with the Ethiopian eunuch, his only instruction was, "Go to that chariot and stay near it" (Acts 8:29). And when the Jerusalem Council weighed and debated whether the Gentiles ought to become circumcised to receive the salvation of Jesus, their letter portrays the Spirit as one of the attendees, quietly helping them to decide the issue. They wrote to the churches, "It seemed good to the Holy Spirit and to us not to burden you" (Acts 15:28). While the Spirit of God is free to bestow whatever miraculous gifts he chooses, I find him very often working in the background to help believers live the Christian life in ways that are holy and honorable.

If the miraculous and ecstatic elements of the Spirit's ministry were so important, so *lasting* for the church, then I would expect to find some systematic instruction about their use in Paul's letters. But it's not there. We don't find Paul saying, "Now, I want to show you how to speak in tongues," or "If you want to prophesy and receive visions, follow these three simple steps." There is no systematic instruction in Paul's letters on the practice of Spirit-gifts. (For that matter, there isn't any instruction on how to use the gifts of helping, administration, or encouraging either.) He does give instruction about speaking in tongues and prophecy, but it's focused mostly on how to curb the abuses that crept in with those practices, not systematic instruction on how to make those things happen. Perhaps there is no instruction on those things because they were so common in the early church. They may have been so commonly understood that no one *needed* instruction on how to use them. But perhaps there is no systematic instruction on using them because Paul didn't expect that they would outlive his generation. Whatever the reason, we simply don't find such instruction.

The Spirit-ual life, as Paul envisioned it, was lived in the power of the Spirit of God. The Spirit was present in the assembly of the local church, joined believers together in heart and mind from great

distances, bestowed gifts to the church for its witness, assisted the
local church and individual believers in prayer, convicted men and
women at the preaching of the gospel, helped discipline wayward
members, and worked in the hearts of believers the common, everyday "fruit" of love, joy, and peace. He continues to do these things
today, and longs to partner with God's people in their maturation.

When "Completion" Comes

We began this project asking the question, "Was Paul spiritual?" and continued to ask of Acts and his letters, "What did this
spirituality look like?" We found Paul to be, as he counseled his
readers to be, a man living by the Spirit of God just like his Lord.

I began this project in the usual way: by reading. I re-read
books on Pauline theology that had formed me in seminary. I
consulted journals and read the latest research in first-century
Greco-Roman history as it pertained to Paul. I bought books on-
line and requested others through interlibrary loan from seminar-
ies and universities all over the United States. The more I read,
the more I wanted to read, and the Paul who had frustrated me
in my youth (and sometimes in my adulthood) came alive again. I
began to see Paul in new and fresh ways, ways that were not always
presented by the authors I was reading. I had always seen Paul as
the guy that you either love or hate. No middle ground with him.
He was intense, smart, educated, and not the kind of man to tell
jokes. He didn't mess around—in his preaching, his pastoring, or
his work—and he didn't tolerate those who did. All of this made
Paul a guy I couldn't relate to, let alone pattern my life after.

On this side of the mountain, though, I see Paul differently.
I see him as a loving, kind-hearted, compassionate man. Intense,
yes—intensely focused on doing what he could to show God's love
(in Christ) to the world. I used to see him as angry, a man who had
"a genius for invective."[3] Now I understand that his anger came

---

3. Tobin, *The Spirituality of Paul*, 14.

from his intense love for his churches and the people in them, and was mostly directed against those who would cause harm to the people he loved or lead them into theological error. Like a man rising to defend his wife's honor, Paul's anger originates in his protective instincts, not his temperament. I see him putting his entire education to use in service of Christ, from his training in rhetoric to his intricate knowledge of the Scriptures. I see him carefully listening to the philosophers on Mars Hill, quietly evaluating their "superstitiousness,"[4] speaking only when it was time. Now that I have four children growing into their teen years, I see Paul as a father (1 Thess. 2:11) and a mother (1 Thess. 2:7), gently caring for his children. My impressions of him are not what they used to be. They've changed a great deal.

It was bound to happen, and I'm not the first one it's happened to. Paul had a reputation in the first century as someone who had a weighty and forceful media persona, but who was soft and unimpressive in reality (2 Cor. 10:10). He knew that he had a tendency to come off stronger and more aggressive in print than he did in person. And for that reason, I wonder if we aren't wise to take the portrait of Paul revealed in his Epistles and dial it back a notch. His letters are impressive, to be sure. The early, extrabiblical records describe Paul as a short man with bowed legs, a bald head, and a big nose,[5] so he may have been physically unimpressive. Yet here was a man who, when he patterned his life after that of Christ Jesus, with the help of the Holy Spirit, turned the world on its head for the glory of Jesus. This gives hope to those of us who read him, who take him seriously, and who want to be spiritual like Paul was.

---

4. One of my seminary professors, Lewis Foster, used to translate the term used in Acts 17:22 (*deisidaimonesterous*) this way.
5. *The Acts of Paul and Thecla* describes him as "a man short in stature, with a bald head, bowed legs, in good condition, eyebrows that met, a fairly large nose, and full of grace." Quoted in Bart Ehrman, *Lost Scriptures: Books That Did Not Make It into the New Testament* (Oxford: University Press, 2003), 114.

The same Spirit who lived in Paul lives in every single believer who belongs to Christ, and he desires and works for the same good, the same honor, the same devotion, the same focused intensity, and the same love that he gave to Paul.

Bibliography

Adler, C. and I. Singer, eds. *The Jewish Encyclopedia*. 5 vols. New York: KTAV Publishing House, 1901.

Allis, Oswald T. *The Unity of Isaiah*. Philadelphia: Presbyterian and Reformed, 1974.

Anderson, Keith R., and Randy D. Reese. *Spiritual Mentoring: A Guide for Seeking and Giving Direction*. Downers Grove, IL: InterVarsity Press, 1999.

Barnett, Paul. *The Second Epistle to the Corinthians*. New International Commentary on the New Testament. Grand Rapids: Eerdmans, 1997.

Barr, James. "Abba Isn't 'Daddy.'" *Journal of Theological Studies* 39 (1988): 28–47.

Barrett, C. K. *Paul: An Introduction to His Thought*. Louisville: Westminster John Knox, 1994.

Bauckham, Richard. *Jesus and the Eyewitnesses: The Gospels as Eyewitness Testimony*. Grand Rapids: Eerdmans, 2006.

Bauer, W., W. F. Arndt, and F. Wilbur Gingrich. *Greek-English Lexicon of the New Testament and Other Early Christian Literature*. 1st and 2nd eds. Chicago: University of Chicago Press, 1957, 1979.

Bauer, W., W. F. Arndt, F. Wilbur Gingrich, and F. W. Danker. *Greek-English Lexicon of the New Testament and Other Early Christian Literature*. 3rd ed. Chicago: University of Chicago Press, 2000.

Best, Ernest. "Paul's Apostolic Authority—?" *Journal for the Study of the New Testament* 9 (Oct. 1986): 3–25.

Black, David Alan. *Using New Testament Greek in Ministry: A Practical Guide for Students and Pastors*. Grand Rapids: Baker, 1993.

Bridges, Jerry. *The Pursuit of Holiness*. Colorado Springs: NavPress, 1978.

Brown, Colin, ed. *New International Dictionary of New Testament Theology*. 4 Vols. Grand Rapids: Zondervan, 1975.

Bruce, F. F. *1 and 2 Corinthians*. New Century Bible. London: Oliphants, 1971.

_____. *Epistle to the Galatians*. New International Greek Testament Commentary. Grand Rapids: Eerdmans, 1982.

_____. *Paul: Apostle of the Heart Set Free*. Grand Rapids: Eerdmans, 1977.

_____. *The Epistles to the Colossians, to Philemon, and to the Ephesians*. New International Commentary on the New Testament. Grand Rapids: Eerdmans, 1984.

_____. *The Pauline Circle*. Grand Rapids: Eerdmans, 1985.

Carter, Warren. *The Roman Empire and the New Testament: An Essential Guide*. Nashville: Abingdon Press, 2006.

Cassuto, U. *A Commentary on the Book of Exodus*. Trans. Israel Abrahams. Jerusalem: Magnes Press, 1983.

Castelli, Elizabeth. *Imitating Paul: A Discourse of Power*. Louisville: Westminster John Knox Press, 1991.

Childs, Brevard. *The Book of Exodus: A Critical Theological Commentary*. Philadelphia: The Westminster Press, 1974.

Cole, R. Alan. *Galatians*. Tyndale New Testament Commentaries. Downers Grove, IL: InterVarsity Press, 2007.

de Caussade, Jean-Pierre. *The Sacrament of the Present Moment*. Trans. Kitty Muggeridge. San Francisco: HarperCollins, 1989.

Deissmann, G. A. *Light from the Ancient East: The New Testament Illustrated by Recently Discovered Texts of the Graeco-Roman World*. Trans. Lionel R. M. Strachan. Peabody, MA: Hendrickson, 1955.

Doberstein, J. "Introduction." In *Life Together* by Dietrich Bonhoeffer. Trans. J. Doberstein. San Francisco: HarperCollins, 1954.

Dunn, James D. G. *Jesus and the Spirit*. Philadelphia: Westminster, 1975.

_____. *The Theology of Paul the Apostle*. Grand Rapids: Eerdmans, 1986.

Edwards, Jonathan. *Jonathan Edwards: Basic Writings*. Ed. O. A. Winslow. New York: The New American Library, 1966.

Ehrman, Bart. *Lost Scriptures: Books That Did Not Make It into the New Testament*. Oxford: University Press, 2003.

Ellis, E. E. "Prophecy in the New Testament Church—and Today." In

Prophetic Vocation in the New Testament and Today. Ed. J. Panagop-
    oulos. Leiden: E. J. Brill, 1977.

Eusebius. *The History of the Church from Christ to Constantine*. Trans. G. A.
    Williamson. New York: Penguin Books, 1965.

Fee, Gordon. *God's Empowering Presence: The Holy Spirit in the Letters of
    Paul*. Peabody, MA: Hendrickson, 1994.

_____. *Paul, the Spirit, and the People of God*. Peabody, MA: Hendrickson,
    1996.

Foster, Richard J. *Celebration of Discipline: The Path to Spiritual Growth*. 3rd
    ed. San Francisco: HarperCollins, 1998.

_____. *Streams of Living Water: Celebrating the Great Traditions of Christian
    Faith*. San Francisco: HarperCollins, 1998.

Friesen, Steven J. *Imperial Cults and the Apocalypse of John*. Oxford: Univer-
    sity Press, 2001.

Furnish, Victor Paul. *The Moral Teaching of Paul*. Nashville: Abingdon, 1979.

Georgi, D. "God Turned Upside Down." In *Paul and Empire: Religion and
    Power in Roman Imperial Society*. Ed. Richard A. Horsley. Harris-
    burg, PA: Trinity Press International, 1997.

Gorman, Michael J. *Apostle of the Crucified Lord: A Theological Introduction
    to Paul and His Letters*. Grand Rapids: Eerdmans, 2004.

_____. *Cruciformity: Paul's Narrative Spirituality of the Cross*. Grand Rap-
    ids: Eerdmans, 2001.

Goulder, Michael. "Vision and Knowledge." *Journal for the Study of the New
    Testament* 17, no. 56 (1995): 53–71.

Green, Joel B., Scot McKnight, and I. Howard Marshall, eds. *Dictionary of
    Jesus and the Gospels*. Downers Grove, IL: InterVarsity Press, 1992.

Hamilton, Victor P. *Handbook on the Pentateuch*. Grand Rapids: Baker, 1982.

Hardin, Leslie T. "Is a Pauline Spirituality Still Viable?" *Journal of Spiritual
    Formation and Soul Care* 8 (2015): 132–146.

_____. "Son of Man." In *The Lexham Bible Dictionary*. Eds. J. D. Barry
    and L. Wentz. Bellingham, WA: Lexham Press, 2012.

_____. "The Quest for the Spiritual Jesus." *Stone-Campbell Journal* 15
    (2012): 217–227.

_____. *The Spirituality of Jesus: Nine Disciplines Jesus Modeled for Us*. Grand Rapids: Kregel, 2009.

Hawthorne, Gerald F., Ralph P. Martin, and Daniel G. Reid, eds. *Dictionary of Paul and His Letters*. Downers Grove, IL: InterVarsity Press, 1993.

Hays, Richard B. *Echoes of Scripture in the Letters of Paul*. New Haven, CT: Yale University Press, 1989.

Henry, Carl F. H. "Spiritual? Say It Isn't So!" in *Alive to God: Studies in Spirituality Presented to James Houston*. Eds. J. I. Packer and Loren Wilkinson. Downers Grove, IL: InterVarsity Press, 1992.

Hock, R. F. "Paul's Tentmaking and the Problem of His Social Class." *Journal of Biblical Literature* 97 (1978): 555–564.

_____. *The Social Context of Paul's Ministry*. Philadelphia: Fortress, 1980.

Hoehner, H. W. *Ephesians: An Exegetical Commentary*. Grand Rapids: Baker, 2002.

Houghton, Felicity B. "Personal Experience of Prayer I." In *Teach Us to Pray: Prayer in the Bible and the World*. Ed. D. A. Carson. Grand Rapids: Baker, 1990.

Howard, Evan. *The Brazos Introduction to Christian Spirituality*. Grand Rapids: Brazos Press, 2008.

Hurtado, Larry. *Lord Jesus Christ: Devotion to Jesus in Earliest Christianity*. Grand Rapids: Eerdmans, 2003.

Irenaeus. *Against Heresies*. In The Ante-Nicene Fathers. Eds. A. R. Roberts and J. Donaldson. Vol. 1. Peabody, MA: Hendrickson, 1999.

Jeremias, J. *The Eucharistic Words of Jesus*. Trans. N. Perrin. Philadelphia: Fortress, 1966.

Jervis, L. Ann. *At the Heart of the Gospel: Suffering in the Earliest Christian Message*. Grand Rapids: Eerdmans, 2007.

Johnson, Luke Timothy. *Religious Experience in Earliest Christianity*. Minneapolis: Fortress Press, 1998.

Jones, Cheslyn, Geoffrey Wainwright, and Edward Yarnold, eds. *The Study of Spirituality*. Oxford: University Press, 1986.

Justin Martyr. *Dialogue with Trypho, A Jew*. In The Ante-Nicene Fathers.

Eds. A. R. Roberts and J. Donaldson. Vol. 1. Peabody, MA: Hendrickson, 1999.

Kaiser, Walter C., Jr. *Mission in the Old Testament: Israel as a Light to the Nations.* Grand Rapids: Baker, 2000.

Keener, Craig. *1-2 Corinthians.* The New Cambridge Bible Commentary. Cambridge: University Press, 2005.

Kittel, G., and G. Friedrich, eds. *Theological Dictionary of the New Testament.* Translated by G. W. Bromiley. 10 vols. Grand Rapids: Eerdmans, 1964-1976.

Knight, George W., III. *The Pastoral Epistles.* New International Greek Testament Commentary. Grand Rapids: Eerdmans, 1992.

Köstenberger, Andreas and Peter O'Brien. *Salvation to the Ends of the Earth: A Biblical Theology of Mission.* New Studies in Biblical Theology. Ed. D. A. Carson. Downers Grove, IL: InterVarsity Press, 2001.

Krause, Mark. "The Lord's Supper in the New Testament." In *Evangelicalism and the Stone-Campbell Movement.* Vol. 2. Ed. William R. Baker. Abilene, TX: ACU Press, 2006.

Liebholz, G. "Memoirs." In *The Cost of Discipleship* by Dietrich Bonhoeffer. Trans. R. H. Fuller and Irmgard Booth. New York: Simon and Schuster, 1959.

Longenecker, Richard N. *The Ministry and Message of Paul.* Grand Rapids: Zondervan, 1971.

Louw, Johannes P. and Eugene A. Nida. *Greek-English Lexicon of the New Testament Based on Semantic Domains.* New York: United Bible Societies, 1989.

MacRae, George W. "Romans 8:26-27." *Interpretation* 34 (1980): 288-292.

Marshall, I. Howard. *Acts.* Tyndale New Testament Commentaries. Grand Rapids: Eerdmans, 1980.

_____. *Last Supper and Lord's Supper.* Grand Rapids: Eerdmans, 1980.

Martin, Ralph. *The Spirit and the Congregation: Studies in 1 Corinthians 12-15.* Grand Rapids: Eerdmans, 1984.

McCant, J. W. "Paul's Thorn of Rejected Apostleship." *New Testament Studies* 34 (1988): 550-572.

McGarvey, J. W. *New Commentary on Acts of Apostles.* 2 Vols. 1892. Reprint, Delight, AR: Gospel Light, n.d.

McKnight, Scot. *A Community Called Atonement.* Living Theology. Ed. Tony Jones. Nashville: Abingdon, 2007.

Meeks, Wayne A. *The First Urban Christians.* New Haven, CT: Yale University Press, 1983.

Merton, Thomas. *Opening the Bible.* Collegeville, MN: The Liturgical Press [1970] 1986.

Murch, James DeForest. *Christians Only: A History of the Restoration Movement.* Cincinnati: Standard Publishing, 1962.

North, Christopher R. *The Suffering Servant in Deutero-Isaiah: An Historical and Critical Study.* Oxford: University Press, 1948.

North, James B. *Union in Truth: An Interpretive History of the Restoration Movement.* Cincinnati: Standard Publishing, 1994.

O'Brien, P. T. *The Letter to the Ephesians.* Pillar New Testament Commentary. Ed. D. A. Carson. Grand Rapids: Eerdmans, 1999.

Ogden, Greg. *Transforming Discipleship: Making Disciples a Few at a Time.* Downers Grove, IL: InterVarsity Press, 2003.

Origen. *Selected Writings.* The Classics of Western Spirituality. Trans. Rowan A. Greer. Mahwah, NJ: Paulist Press, 1979.

Osborne, Robert E. "Paul and the Wild Beasts." *Journal of Biblical Literature* 85, no. 2 (1966): 225-230.

Oswalt, John N. *Isaiah Chapters 40-66.* Grand Rapids: Eerdmans, 1998.

Page, Sydney H. T. "The Suffering Servant between the Testaments." *New Testament Studies* 31 (1985): 481-497.

Peterson, Eugene H. *Eat This Book: A Conversation in the Art of Spiritual Reading.* Grand Rapids: Eerdmans, 2006.

_____. *The Jesus Way.* Grand Rapids: Eerdmans, 2007.

_____. *The Wisdom of Each Other.* Grand Rapids: Zondervan, 1998.

Quinn, J. D. "The Last Volume of Luke: The Relation of Luke-Acts to the Pastoral Epistles." In *Perspectives on Luke-Acts.* Ed. Charles

H. Talbert. Danville, VA: Association of Baptist Professors of Religion, 1978.

Roose, Kevin. *The Unlikely Disciple: A Sinner's Semester at America's Holiest University*. New York: Grand Central Publishing, 2009.

Sanders, E. P. *Paul and Palestinian Judaism*. Philadelphia: Fortress, 1977.

Sandnes, K. O. *Paul–One of the Prophets?* Wissenschaftliche Untersuchungen zum Neuen Testament. Vol. 2, 43. Tübingen: Mohr-Siebeck, 1991.

Schnabel, Eckhard. *Early Christian Mission*. 2 Vols. Downers Grove, IL: InterVarsity Press, 2004.

Skeat, T. C. "'Especially the Parchments': A Note on 2 Timothy 4:13." *Journal of Theological Studies* 30 (1979): 173-177.

Smith, Christian. *The Bible Made Impossible: Why Biblicism Is Not a Truly Evangelical Reading of Scripture*. Grand Rapids: Brazos Press, 2011.

Spencer, William David and Aida Besançon Spencer. *The Prayer Life of Jesus: Shout of Agony, Revelation of Love, a Commentary*. Lanham, MD: University Press of America, 1990.

Stanley, David M. *Boasting in the Lord: The Phenomenon of Prayer in Saint Paul*. New York: Paulist Press, 1973

Stendahl, Krister. "Paul at Prayer." *Interpretation* 34 (1980): 240-249.

Stowers, Stanley. *Letter Writing in Greco-Roman Antiquity*. Library of Early Christianity. Ed. Wayne A. Meeks. Philadelphia: Westminster, 1986.

Tertullian. *Against Marcion*. In The Ante-Nicene Fathers. Ed. A. R. Roberts and J. Donaldson. Vol. 3. Peabody, MA: Hendrickson, 1999.

Thiselton, Anthony C. *First Corinthians: A Shorter and Exegetical Commentary*. Grand Rapids: Eerdmans, 2006.

_____. *The First Epistle to the Corinthians*. The New International Greek Testament Commentary. Grand Rapids: Eerdmans, 2000.

_____. *The Living Paul: An Introduction to the Apostle's Life and Thought*. Downers Grove, IL: InterVarsity Press, 2009.

Thurston, Bonnie Bowman. "'Caught Up to the Third Heavens' and

'Helped by the Spirit': Paul and the Mystery of Prayer." *Stone-Campbell Journal* 11 (2008): 223–233.

Tidball, Derek. *The Message of Holiness*. Downers Grove, IL: InterVarsity Press, 2010.

Tobin, Thomas H. *The Spirituality of Paul*. Eugene, OR: Wipf and Stock, 1987.

Turner, Max. *The Holy Spirit and Spiritual Gifts*. Peabody, MA: Hendrickson, 1996.

van der Horst, Pieter W. "Silent Prayer in Antiquity." *Numen* 41 (1994): 1–25.

Weatherly, Jon A. "The Role of Baptism in Conversion: Israel's Promises Fulfilled for the Believer in Jesus." In *Evangelicalism and the Stone-Campbell Movement*. Vol. 1. Ed. William R. Baker. Downers Grove, IL: InterVarsity Press, 2002.

Wenham, David. *Paul: Follower of Jesus or Founder of Christianity?* Grand Rapids: Eerdmans, 1995.

Wiles, Gordon P. *Paul's Intercessory Prayers: The Significance of the Intercessory Prayer Passages in the Letters of St. Paul*. Cambridge: Cambridge University Press, 1974.

Willard, Dallas. *Renovation of the Heart*. Colorado Springs: NavPress, 2002.

Witherington, Ben, III. *The Paul Quest: The Renewed Search for the Jew of Tarsus*. Downers Grove, IL: InterVarsity Press, 1998.

Wright, N. T. *Jesus and the Victory of God*. Minneapolis: Fortress, 1996.

———. *Justification: God's Plan and Paul's Vision*. Downers Grove, IL: InterVarsity Press, 2009.

———. *Paul: In Fresh Perspective*. Minneapolis: Fortress, 2005.

———. *The Climax of the Covenant: Christ and the Law in Pauline Theology*. Minneapolis: Fortress, 1993.

Yancey, Philip. *The Jesus I Never Knew*. Grand Rapids: Zondervan, 1995.

Young, Brad H. *Meet the Rabbis: Rabbinic Thought and the Teachings of Jesus*. Peabody, MA: Hendrickson, 2007.